VOICES FROM STATE

An Oral History of Arkansas State University

Arkansas State University
State University, Arkansas 72467

Library of Congress Cataloging in Publication Data:

Ball, Larry D., 1940-
Voices from State.

"A 75th anniversary publication of Arkansas State
University."
1. Arkansas State University—History. I. Clements,
William M., 1945-   . II. Arkansas State University.
III. Title.
LD245.B34   1984   378.767'98   84-14528

ISBN 0-930677-00-5
Printed in the United States of America

VOICES FROM STATE

An Oral History of Arkansas State University

By Larry D. Ball and William M. Clements

A 75th Anniversary Publication
of Arkansas State University
1984

*To all who have contributed
to the growth of Arkansas State University
and the advancement of
higher education for the Mid-South*

PREFACE

Leland W. "Tex" Plunkett, former A-State student and faculty member and master raconteur, tells the following story about V.C. Kays, the first president of what is now Arkansas State University:

" You never could tell where Mr. Kays was going to show up. He would show up anywhere, day or night, the most unusual places. This story was told when I first came here as a freshman. The story is about how Mr. Kays got his limp. [In] Barnhart dorm, which was a girls' dorm three stories tall, Mrs. Warr was in charge of the cafeteria. They served family-style meals then. You could eat all you wanted to. She was in charge of meals and was a very industrious woman, but she was getting up in years. They had attached a pulley to the eaves of Barnhart Hall and attached a basket where she would put her laundry and pull it up. Oftentimes at night, these girls being in so early felt the need of masculine company. So a boyfriend would get into the basket and give a signal, and they would pull the boy up. The story goes that Mr. Kays heard what was going on and learned the signal and got into the basket. And the girls pulled him up and looked out the window and saw who they had and turned the rope loose. **"**

When Plunkett told us this story during a tape-recorded interview, he prefaced and concluded it with doubts of its factual accuracy. But at the same time he saw it as revealing the nature of President Kays' involvement with students who were attending the institution to which he had dedicated so much of his life. "I don't know if that story is true," Plunkett said, "but if you knew Mr. Kays, you could well believe it."

Plunkett's story, versions of which we heard from three other interviewees, reflects both the weaknesses and strengths of the oral account as historical document and of the storyteller as repository of historical data. On one hand, the oral account frequently lacks the factual accuracy that printed documents are more likely to possess. Reasons for this lack are obvious and manifold. For example, when a story is retold several times, perhaps with lengthy periods of time separating the retellings, details of the event upon which the story is based may be forgotten. In a print- and media-oriented society, oral accounts may be especially prone to lapses. Even when outlines of an event persist, details such as dates, precise locations, and names of participants may disappear. An effective storyteller will often make substitutions for forgotten material so that the tale will be as interesting for listeners as possible. In fact, the better storyteller is more likely to sacrifice factual accuracy for literary effect: condensing plot, intensifying conflict, couching direct discourse in colorful diction, focusing on distinctive traits in the personalities of the story's characters.

Yet this does not mean that oral accounts are worthless as historical data. In many cases, they provide the only sources of information on some subjects. Indeed, the history of an institution such as Arkansas State would exhibit many gaps if the oral record were not tapped. Oral history alone preserves the memory of Fannie Cash, the black cook at "Aggie" during the late teens and early twenties; of the logistics of balancing heavy schedules of classes, working, and social life during the Depression years at Arkansas State College during the 1930s; of the dilemmas raised by the influx of World War II veterans on the GI Bill during the late 1940s; and of the intricate maneuverings in Little Rock during the 1960s that culminated in university status for Arkansas State.

One may argue that the factual material in oral history becomes blurred and distorted by the peculiar perspectives and prejudices of the storytellers. While such a charge cannot be dismissed (it also applies to the compilers of historical documents), the bias that each storyteller brings to the material constitutes one of the strengths of oral history. For the oral narrative or description provides a glimpse of history at a very personal level. After all, every historical event has affected those who were involved in it as participant or observer. The nature of the effect depends upon each person's interpretation.

Thus, while Plunkett's narrative about President Kays in the laundry basket lacks some documentary precision since it omits such information as the date of the occurrence, names of the young women involved, and repercussions the incident caused, it offers an insight into the way Plunkett and others of his generation of storytellers viewed Arkansas State's paternalistic first president. It also affords some insight into rules imposed by the institution on its students, as well as into the mores of northeast Arkansas in the 1930s when Plunkett was a college student. Even if a folklorist regards the story as a timeless jest, thus denying its factuality, the account has value for the history of Arkansas State as a mirror of student attitudes about their school. As oral history, stories such as this one contribute significantly to a fuller view of the development of the institution of higher education that became Arkansas State University.

In the summer of 1979, Arkansas State University established the Mid-South Center for Oral History for gathering through tape-recorded interviews the reminiscences of persons who had figured in the history of the region as participants or observers. The center's first project was an oral history of the university itself. We felt that such an undertaking was particularly significant, given the institution's rapid growth from an agricultural high school to a major regional university. Moreover, since persons were still living who remembered the school's beginnings and who had attended classes during its earliest years, the time for such a project seemed ripe and perhaps urgent. Consequently, we concentrated on interviewing people who had been associated with the university as students, faculty, administrators, or support staff. In selecting interviewees, our intent was to be as representative as possible—that is, to include a variety of associations with Arkansas State as well as coverage of all chronological periods. While most of the interviews were completed during the fall semester of 1979, interviewing for the project continued through spring 1984. The collected reminiscences comprise numerous hours of tape, all of which is on deposit and available for public use in the Dean B. Ellis Library at Arkansas State University.

As we were doing our oral history research, we were aware of the fine documentary history prepared by Lee A. Dew, *The ASU Story: A History of Arkansas State University, 1909-1967* (State College: ASU Press, 1968). We do not think of our efforts as supplanting Dew's work in any way. Instead, we are presenting the personal side of Arkansas State's history, which complements Dew's excellently researched treatment of a more official aspect of the institution's development. Thus, our work, though it brings the "ASU story" to a more recent date than Dew was able to do, in no way supersedes his work. Both books should be read to get a full picture of Arkansas State's history. The reader who is most interested in the factual history of the institution's development should go to Dew's book first; the reader who wishes to share vicariously the experiences of those who participated in that history should come to ours.

An oral history is not "complete" until everyone connected in any way with the subject has been interviewed. Such is certainly impossible with our subject. But we have attempted to interview a meaningful cross-section of people who have known Arkansas State at various points in its history. The following pages present a selection of their memories. For the most part, we have left those memories in the words of the interviewees. Occasionally this makes for difficulties in reading. After all, none of us speaks in the unbroken flow of words in which the prose stylist writes. But we believe that since this volume is primarily the product of the memories and storytelling artistry of the interviewees, they

should have their say exactly as they said it. The chronologically arranged chapters that follow are oral history. As such, accuracy may occasionally be found wanting (though we have tried to avoid egregious errors in fact), but we think that the personal side of history as lived by articulate individuals compensates for any departures from a more conventional historical presentation.

ACKNOWLEDGMENTS

Many individuals and agencies contributed to the preparation of this book. Of course, our primary debt is to the interviewees, who graciously granted us time for long, sometimes strenuous tape-recorded conferences. Their words appear throughout the text, and they are recognized individually in Appendix A, along with the date of interview. Rarely do researchers have the opportunity to consult persons associated with the formation of a school such as Arkansas State that has grown into a university in such a short time.

Photographs in the volume, which convey the history of ASU in parallel to the text, derive from a number of sources. We wish to thank these donors, listed in the picture credits (Appendix B), who have loaned their photographic treasures to complement the oral memories of the interviewees. Many of these photographs will be deposited in the ASU Museum.

We also are grateful to the Arkansas State College (Kays) Foundation and to the Arkansas Endowment for the Humanities (AEH). The foundation provided funds for equipment and supplies to establish the Mid-South Center for Oral History, and the research for this oral history of ASU was carried out through the center. The AEH awarded a grant that allowed us some time off from teaching schedules to conduct most of the initial research for this volume.

Various departments and offices of Arkansas State University have assisted in many ways—through reassignment of teaching time for the authors and through substantial clerical, computer, and transcription services. While many individuals have assisted in the mechanical aspects of producing the manuscript for this book, we particularly thank Dianne Bufford for her long hours of transcription, typing, and retyping.

We have received valuable advice and criticism from the Editorial Advisory Committee, a group of staff members and alumni who took time from their busy schedules to read and evaluate the early drafts of the manuscript and provide other editorial assistance. The committee included Ruth Hawkins, J. William Berry, Lena French, George Horneker, Ron Looney, Tom Manning, Steven McFerron, and Walter Strong.

Ruth Hawkins has been a careful editor and judicious critic of the manuscript at every stage. Her suggestions have helped us round out this story of the growth of ASU. Ron Looney and Tom Manning have contributed their insights, both into the history of the institution and into the production of the manuscript. Cynthia Livingston created the design for the book, ably integrating text and photographs.

We also appreciate the financial contributions provided to the university by the Arkansas State College Foundation and V.H. Kays to assist in production of this book.

Enthusiasm for this project from various quarters of the university and its community has been overwhelming. This ardor has helped to sustain us through the tribulations that invariably arise in the preparation of such a volume. Many have influenced this book in many ways; it should be considered a communal undertaking. We gratefully acknowledge the assistance we have received.

CHAPTER I

"THINGS STARTED AT AN ELEMENTAL LEVEL"
The Agricultural High School Phase

O n April 1, 1909, Governor
George W. Donaghey signed legislation that
significantly influenced the lives of the people of
Arkansas. This law, Act 100, created four "public
schools of agriculture" within the state, one in
each of four districts. Although this law
envisioned only institutions of high school rank,
they were to instruct students in "agriculture,
horticulture, and the art of textile making," all
areas in which Arkansans were sadly lacking in
knowledge. To obtain an education in agriculture
in Arkansas was difficult, if not impossible.
William Troy Martin, who grew up in eastern
Arkansas early in this century, recalled this
problem:

66 Previous to 1910, there [were] only two
state supported educational institutions in the
State of Arkansas. [They were] the University of
Arkansas and what they called Normal School at
Conway [now University of Central Arkansas].
. . . At that particular time the University of
Arkansas' so-called College of Agriculture was not
accredited. . . . And so if a boy or girl desired an
education in agriculture, you had to go outside
the state. **99**

Much of the agitation for the creation of new
agricultural schools in Arkansas came from the
Farmers' Union movement. This statewide
organization—with nationwide links—proposed to
advance not only the political position of farmers
in Arkansas, but their economic and social
standing as well. An educated agricultural
community held a prominent place in the plans of
the Farmers' Union. E. Roy Keller, who like
Martin grew up in eastern Arkansas, remembered

In August 1910, the board of trustees let the contract for
the original Administration Building to Monk and Richie,
Contractors, of Pine Bluff for $29,080. The firm was
given six months to complete the job. The building faced
south, toward the railroad tracks, since many students
arrived by rail. A fence ran along the back of the building,
and the Aggie herd was allowed to graze on the front
lawn.

*The first classes of the State Agricultural School met in
the old Elks Lodge at the corner of Main and Washington
streets in downtown Jonesboro. Classes were held in the
building temporarily while a campus was being constructed east of town on the old Warner-Krewson
estate.*

President Kays introduced to northeast Arkansas the principle that barns should be substantial. The large dairy barn, located south of the present post office, featured a hipped roof that was widely acclaimed.

that his father played an important part in this farmers' organization:

❝ My father was very much interested in education, [especially] rural—[and to] see that every child went to consolidated schools. He went to Little Rock to the state Farmers' Union meeting when they had 75,000 members. He introduced a resolution asking the governor and the state legislature to create these four agricultural schools. . . . Ike Doyle's father seconded the motion, and they were put on a legislative committee to lobby that [resolution] through the governor and legislature. It went to the governor's office first, and the governor was very cordial and fine. . . . Daddy said they jumped on him [the governor] like a duck on a june bug, and [he] said, 'Boys, I'll help you put that through the legislature.' And they did, and it went through with a whoop through the Arkansas legislature. ❞

Many communities began to demand one of the schools in or near their city. With only four institutions provided for in the act, the rivalry was keen. In the First District, which included Paragould, Mountain Home, and Jonesboro among other towns, the competition was especially fervent. Many chapters of the Farmers' Union in northeastern Arkansas reportedly desired Jonesboro as the site for one of the schools. Within days of passage of Act 100, an advertising and soliciting campaign was underway. Robert Fulton Barnett resided in Jonesboro at that time and recalled this fund drive:

❝ On the side of a building right up here on Huntington Avenue there was a bank on the . . . southwest corner. And on that bank they had a sign that must have been thirty feet long. In large letters it said, 'Will we have the Agricultural School?' 'It's up to us' was written in smaller letters on an angle on each end. ❞

Barnett also encountered one of the fund-raisers, E.C. Barton, owner of a lumber company. "Bob, do you want to help on the donation to this fund?" queried Barton firmly. Barnett signed some notes and "finally paid them."

The fund drive provoked discord in some local households. Lebelva Connelly, then a young girl, overheard an argument between her father and mother:

❝ My mother was very angry at my father, who was donating money to bring an A&M College to this part of the country. She said, 'You have two little girls. What in the world do you want with an Agricultural and Mechanical College?' My father explained that, 'you see you have to have backing of different interests to get them to locate here.' And he explained that 'since we live off the farmlands and since we live in Jonesboro, we own a home here, everything that improves is an advantage for our girls regardless [if] they ever go there or not.' ❞

Mr. and Mrs. C.V. Warr, the first two employees hired after Kays assumed his duties, were given living quarters in the Girls' Dormitory as part of their compensation. Their daughter, Margaret, poses on the lawn shortly after the dorm was completed and the family took up residence.

The Girls' Dormitory was renamed Barnhart Hall around 1930 in honor of Edith Barnhart, dean of women during the 1920s.

Two residence halls were among the first buildings completed on campus. They were referred to simply as the Girls' Dormitory and the Boys' Dormitory for many years. This Boys' Dormitory, slightly larger than its companion, was eventually renamed Lewis Hall in recognition of J.B. "Dad" Lewis, the Craighead County representative on the original board of trustees.

The farsightedness of such citizens enabled the community to raise $40,000 as a bid for the new high school. On March 28, 1910, the newly appointed board of trustees decided in favor of Jonesboro as the site for the institution. In addition to the $40,000, a pledge of 200 acres of land was included.

While the promoters of the agricultural school were busily seeking funds, State Senator C.E. Bush, one of the trustees, investigated programs of various colleges in the South and sought a principal for the new school at Jonesboro. While on the campus of the agricultural school in Wetumpka, Alabama, Bush met Victor Cicero Kays, agricultural director of that academy. Bush offered him the principalship, and Kays accepted. Kays was a member of a farm family from Illinois. Since the 1830s, his ancestors had tilled the soil on the Little Oxbow Prairie some forty miles north of Peoria. As Victor H. "Buddy" Kays (son of V.C. Kays) declared, the family farm "was managed in a progressive manner. That was the atmosphere that he [V.C. Kays] grew up in":

66 In those days they had trouble with wheat rust, and my grandfather brought in the seed resistant to that [disease] direct from Russia. Their Jersey herd was brought in direct from the Isle of Jersey. Later on when Daddy was still at the University of Illinois, just before he graduated my grandfather died, and he had to go home and take care of the farm. . . . And then, when one of his brothers succeeded him, he started the soil surveys—really before the University of Illinois got into soil surveys. The first hybrid corn in that area was planted on that [family] farm. So that farm has always been in the lead on those things. . . . And he brought those traits with him. 99

V.C. Kays possessed impressive credentials for his task at the new agricultural school. Only twenty-eight years of age in 1910, he held a bachelor's degree from Northern Illinois State Teachers College in DeKalb and a second degree in science from the University of Illinois at Urbana. While teaching at the State College of Agriculture in Las Cruces, New Mexico, he earned another bachelor's and a master's degree.

For a brief time, he worked as a chemist in the experimental station in nearby Mesilla Park before going on to Wetumpka, Alabama. The board of trustees of the State Agricultural School at Jonesboro formally appointed V.C. Kays as principal on June 1, 1910.

The next few months were busy ones for Kays and his small staff, which included C.V. Warr, farm superintendent, and Warr's wife, Lucille, as matron of dormitories. The principal had not only the task of arranging for immediate classes, but also that of constructing a new and permanent campus. He arranged temporary quarters in the old Elks Lodge building at the corner of Washington and Main streets in downtown Jonesboro, with dormitories in nearby rental property. Edgar Kirk, who worked for "Mother" Warr as a student in the 1930s, recalled her stories about the problems of providing services:

❝ She said she had a big wood-burning range in the room that was to be the kitchen. And so far as any dormitory accommodations, all they had was a bunch of mattresses to throw down on the floor for the students. Somehow or other she got a meal prepared the first afternoon. **❞**

Students soon began to arrive in Jonesboro, eager to take advantage of the first session of the new school in 1910. William Troy Martin learned about this budding seat of learning through the first school catalog. Martin's uncle—an active member of the Farmers' Union—received the catalog and passed it on to the young man. The prospective student arrived in Jonesboro but had some difficulty locating either Principal Kays or the school:

❝ When I got off the train at Jonesboro, I started walking up Main Street, stopping at different stores and inquiring where the college was located. I was surprised that a number of them didn't know anything about it—didn't know they had a college in the city. I continued on, and I began to get discouraged. So I went to the post office and asked where Mr. Kays was rooming. They told me over at the old Parsons Hotel. So I went over there, and they told me

that he wasn't there, but that he was up at the school. They told me how to get there, and . . . I found the school was located on the corner of Washington and Main on the second story of several business houses. I found Mr. Kays in consultation with H.M. Cooley, who was the attorney for the college at that time, and I told him who I was and what I was there for. **❞**

While classes were getting underway, Kays supervised the construction of the permanent buildings on the spacious acreage one and one-half miles east of Jonesboro. He chose a site near several railroads: the Saint Louis and San Francisco; the Saint Louis and Southwestern; and the Jonesboro, Lake City and Eastern. The immediate site was, in the words of Mother Warr, a "gullied, persimmon-thicketed hill," but the location near a railroad was essential, since asphalt highways and motor vehicles were things of the future.

Vegetable gardening classes at Aggie studied hotbed and cold frame methods. The man on his knees bedding sweet potatoes is the school's gardener, J.A. Sammons. Thanks to special soil-building techniques, the campus potato patch produced outstanding yields each year.

Many delays hindered the construction of the first structure, the central building of the new campus. Although the profits would be substantial to a contractor, Kays had some difficulty in locating a willing group of laborers. Buddy Kays related the reasons:

❝ Well, this was an old farm, and I don't know how long before the site was picked, but several months maybe a year or two. . . there had been a lynching up here by where one of the girls' dormitories is now. . . . What the lynching was over, I don't know. But when the contractor moved in, he couldn't get any local blacks to work for him out here on the labor crews, so he imported a crew from, I believe, Pine Bluff. **❞**

The Aggie Girls Glee Club of 1912-13, directed by Pearl Sidenius (front center in top photo), made it evident quite early that female students were interested in learning more than home economics.

Transportation in the early days often was provided by Sally the Mule and her cart. When Sally wasn't transporting students, she pulled the garbage wagon or the plow.

While not so imposing, the barn occupied a prominent place in the scheme of instruction. In a region where barns were often mere shanties and livestock were exposed to the elements, the principal and his staff desired to demonstrate the value of sturdy modern barns. Buddy Kays remembered the original structure with fondness:

66 Then they built what I call the 'old barn.' It was an L-shaped building. Where the show ring was, the two legs of the L met. And it had a nice hipped roof that was later . . . roofed over with asbestos shingles. And for a while Johns-Mansville used that roof in their advertising because of the lines of it . . . . That's located right where the post office is now, in that area. And you had stanchions in both wings of the barn. There were classrooms in the barn. In fact, there was one big classroom upstairs—and an amphitheater effect with seats upon the steps. The hay was stored up in the haylofts. 99

The original charge to the State Agricultural School was to prepare male students for more productive farming and females for wiser management of the home. But additional purposes soon became apparent—among them, the preparation of students for entry into four-year colleges and universities. Within a short time, Aggie offered a two-year course at the junior college level. Graduates of this latter program were accepted into universities at the junior class ranking. In addition, Aggie boasted a literary department, music department, art department, and commercial department. The first graduating class—five persons—received diplomas in May 1913.

Some confusion has occurred in regard to the earliest graduating classes. The misunderstanding apparently results from the fact that Aggie matriculated high school students and simultaneously offered junior college courses. It was not until 1918 that the legislature formally elevated the school to the status of a junior college. William Troy Martin was graduated from the junior college program before World War I and was then accepted by the University of Illinois as a junior. Said Martin:

I finished up my high school work there and had two years of college. We had chemistry, we had soil physics, soil chemistry. We had botany, zoology, entomology, livestock judging, and livestock textbooks on breeds and breeding and so forth, feeds and feeding. Most of these texts were written by the faculty at the University of Illinois. . . . And we had agronomy, field crops, in addition to those other subjects I mentioned. When we finished that, Mr. Kays got in a hurry for a graduating class, so we got together three boys and two girls to graduate in 1913. **"**

These students received much practical instruction outside the classroom. Service on a stock judging team offered students an opportunity to see parts of the nation they otherwise would not have visited. Aggie soon won applause for its keen-eyed judges. Martin served on several judging teams:

" I was also a member of the first stock judging team coached by Mr. [S.H.] Ray. The team members consisted of Frank W. Farley, [Earlie] Elliott, Joe Burns, and [others]. . . . We went to Fort Worth, Texas, to the Fat Stock Show. We competed against Texas A&M, Oklahoma A&M, and it seems like it was New Mexico. I'm not sure what other state. But we were not on the bottom. I think we were second. So that indicates the quality of training that we had in Jonesboro at that particular time. **"**

All students were required to work for room and board. The pay—fifteen cents an hour—might seem paltry today, but this meager sum was sufficient in the early decades of this century. E. Roy Keller, who attended the State Agricultural School with Martin, participated grudgingly in the work program:

" They had the foolish idea that we had to work a half a day on the farm to get practical experience on a farm. Well, they soon found out I [had] filled silo[s] and done everything else they did out here, fence building and caring for livestock at my own farm, my own home four miles southwest of Jonesboro. So they named me foreman. They had a farm superintendent

here, and they worked us on shifts, Monday, Tuesday, through Friday. . . . The boys worked, a fifth of them each day, and the girls worked, a fifth, at the dorms doing laundry and learning how to do things over there. **"**

Later, Keller drove the mail hack to and from Jonesboro. He enjoyed this duty much more than farm work:

" We didn't have a paved road and very poor gravel roads from here to the post office. I hauled students out here in the morning and took them home at night when I took the mail in a mule team hack. I knew about all the professors' love affairs from special delivery, and all like that. Kept it in confidence, of course. **"**

As the students reluctantly undertook their work details, they were often joined by Principal Kays. Keller was surprised to see him join in an exercise in concrete mixing one day:

" Mr. Kays would show us how to mix concrete with a shovel, you know, how to make it easy—scoot the shovel under the concrete and let it rest on the corner of the shovel and flip it over. Mix it better and then they could shovel it. Easier, too. He showed us how to do that. And how to stretch fence posts and a lot of other things that he would do. . . . He knew how to farm. He was an administrator. He knew how to inspire and motivate teachers and students. **"**

While study and manual labor took much time, the inventive student also found time for recreation. Several athletic teams appeared almost simultaneously with the campus. Martin and his classmates organized football and basketball teams in 1911. Frank Parks coached both sports. Martin, who played right tackle, recalled that the rules were very different in those days:

" At that particular time, there was not such a thing as a forward pass. You either had to kick or carry the ball. Roy Keller was a guard and I would stand on the right side, right of the center, and we made it up when the player was called to

Aggie's first football team included (front row, left to right) Raymond Reese, Frank W. Farley, Spurgeon Clark, Lawrence Lambert, William Troy Martin, E. Roy Keller, Will Turner; (back row) Coach Frank Parks, Joe Burns, King Banks, Willie Bernard, and John Evans.

The 1911 basketball team gained a reputation for winning "squeakers." Left to right are Coach Frank Parks, Joe Burns, John Evans, Guy Cobb, Fred Barnett, Will Turner, and Raymond Reese. Athletes were responsible for providing their own uniforms.

The 1912-13 baseball team included (seated from left) Foy Hammons, Oral McCall, Troy Martin, Charlie Whitaker, Henry Vicry; (standing from left) Coach Farr, Raymond Reese, Val Hershberger, Bishop McCork, James Skillern, and Oley Clark.

come through us. We would then follow it and grab our opponents around the ankles so that they would fall on us and the ball could not go through. We did that until they caught us at it and stopped us, of course. There was only one official. **"**

The Aggie basketball team won some notoriety in its first season and began a tradition of winning "squeakers." Keller participated in a tight game against a group of Memphis opponents:

" We were playing my junior year in Memphis, and we had four minutes left in the game and we were six points behind. We had a center, Foy Hammons. He was a coach here later. . . . He took my place at center, and I was glad to get out of the spot and get moved to forward because center was a hard job, jumping all the time—every time either side made a goal. So we got in a huddle, and I said . . . 'Give Raymond Reese four tip-ups, and I'll make four field goals. I'll tie the score in three minutes, and I'll win the game with the other goal.' Two minutes and fifty seconds, I had the game tied and he passed another ball to me, and I won the game by two points. **"**

Principal V.C. Kays followed his youthful teams regularly and often assisted his coaches. As an athlete and former baseball coach in New Mexico, Kays, recalled Keller, "would come down with the coach and give us a little pep talk." Keller thought the presence of the school official "was very unusual," and the teams actually "had two coaches instead of one in all the games I played." The principal showed considerable interest in his athletes. On one occasion, he enabled basketball player Fred Barnett to make a game trip to Little Rock by giving the player his own railroad pass.

These young athletes played with only the most rudimentary equipment. Barnett remembered, "They didn't have any clothes at all for us" basketball players. "We had to rummage around and get our suits and shoes and stockings, everything." Even the selection of school colors required a committee. Martin and

Among the faculty in 1912-13 were (front row, left to right) Frank Parks, Mary Efale Brown, Henry Ness, S.H. (Jack) Ray; (second row) Nira Beck, D.R. Jennings; (third row) V.C. Kays, Arthur Barrett, and Zenobia Brumbaugh.

11

Zenobia Brumbaugh, the art and economics teacher, were among the members. Martin did not recall what prompted the committee to select red and black, but that was the decision. "The athletic teams were called 'Aggies,'" said Martin.

One of the purposes of academic life at Aggie was to instill discipline in the student body. V.C. Kays imposed a stern code of moral conduct. Regulations guided their daily routines. Martin remembered that "discipline was very strict":

“ The boys were not allowed to date the girls except on maybe Friday night and Saturday night, and when they did, they had to go in a group with a chaperone. I met the date at the girls' dormitory in the parlor and had to have a chaperone present. So in going to and from the school through the dining room and back and forth, we were not allowed to walk beside a girl. We had to walk so many paces in front or in back of the girl. . . . And another thing. No cigarettes were allowed to be smoked inside the building, and, of course, no girls smoked cigarettes. Mr. Kays made the rule that you could not smoke in the dormitory. So if I smelled smoke [Martin was a dorm manager], I had to find out where it was. ”

The vigilant school director also forbade his athletes from smoking or drinking alcoholic beverages. Much to Keller's surprise, Kays "even had the boys sign a pledge that they wouldn't have anything to do with the girls of ill-fame!"

Such a problem did exist in turn-of-the-century Jonesboro. Several houses of prostitution flourished and, needless to say, the young students of the State Agricultural School were easy prey for the more experienced women of the night. Buddy Kays later heard the story of his father's struggle to protect his wards from these temptations. First, the elder Kays extracted a verbal agreement from the owners of the nightspots that they would refuse admission to the students. The owners promptly violated this arrangement. When Kays approached the city lawmen, they appeared to be in league with the houses of prostitution. Kays and the school attorney, H.M. Cooley, then employed an

operative of the Pinkerton National Detective Agency of Chicago to gather evidence against the houses of prostitution. Buddy Kays related the rest of the story:

“ They called a meeting of the 'leading citizens' in the YMCA uptown and announced what they had done and what they were about to do [to prosecute], and some of them [silent supporters of the prostitutes] started talking. Oh, couldn't they pray with these poor people and reform them and so on? But some of those folks were talking this way [because of] the property those folks were renting from them. That's pretty good rental because it's in cash and two or three times what the rental value is. I don't know, I've always had just a little bit of doubt about some of those good folks. Anyhow, they cleaned the town up. ”

For the coeds, life could be very confining, and school authorities were especially protective. It was a joyous occasion when the female students obtained permission to go downtown on a weekend. Mother Warr later informed Edgar Kirk:

“ . . .how that in the early days the girls were allowed to go to town, I believe, maybe on a Saturday, chaperoned . . . how that they'd stand as many girls as could be stood in the wagon. It was an old farm wagon with the high sideboards on. Hitch four horses to the wagon and drag it down Aggie Road to town in the wintertime. The mud would be so deep that the hubs would drag on the road as they rolled up Aggie Road to town. ”

Aggie homecoming parades became annual events on Main Street in downtown Jonesboro. Miss Liberty, portrayed by Lela Jane Bryan (with crown), presided over the "Ship of State" float in the 1911 parade.

livestock is better than theirs or not, and they'll ask questions. And like anything else, if it's their idea, they'll follow it through much better than if it's somebody else's idea. So that was one method they used to get things started around here. **"**

This sense of mission set the school apart from Jonesboro and vicinity. By urging students to embrace notions often contrary to or different from their parents' attitudes, a tension soon arose. This tension—sometimes called "town-gown rivalry"—often translated into political competition, a contest for position that appeared very shortly after Aggie opened in 1910. The citizens of Jonesboro quickly attempted to moderate this "alien" influence by placing their own people on the faculty of the school. William Troy Martin observed this rivalry in action:

" Politicians in Jonesboro felt they should run the school. They began to put the pressure on Mr. Kays to hire just local people to teach here. . . . Well, he refused. He hired his faculties from different universities. The head of the animal husbandry was from Ames, Iowa, and the head of the agronomy department was from Ames, also. . . . Mr. [W.H.] Black—head of the animal husbandry department—resigned after one year, and he was succeeded by Mr. [S.H.] Ray from Texas A&M. **"**

The principal desired good relations with the community. When qualified faculty were available from the local schools, he employed them. But, as Martin pointed out, the townspeople went to some lengths to place more persons on the faculty:

" They started fighting Mr. Kays, and through the Farm Bureau and the politicians in Jonesboro, and it got so strong that they would have investigations of the school. And the Farm Bureau managed to get one of their members on the board, Mr. [J.A.] Blackford . . . and he was out making speeches fighting the school, not the school, but Mr. Kays. He was trying to get rid of Mr. Kays. After he [Blackford] was appointed to the board, Mr. Kays took him in and showed him

how the school was operated, opened the books and showed him how the finances were handled. **"**

Although the principal's books satisified Blackford, members of the Farm Bureau persisted in their efforts to control Aggie. According to Martin, the bureau attempted to persuade the legislature to place all four agricultural schools under the supervision of the University of Arkansas. This effort failed when Kays persuaded the other presidents that the four district agricultural schools should work together for their common good.

These problems soon receded into the background as the threat of World War I engulfed the United States. Although President Woodrow Wilson avoided the commitment of American forces for three years, from 1914 to 1917, the threat presented by the German Empire became inescapable. The faculty, staff, and students of the new agricultural school in remote northeastern Arkansas now had the task of supporting the war effort. The institution had weathered the usual birthing pangs and possessed a dedicated, though small, staff and student body. Although the relative isolation of its setting and the indifference—often hostility—of some northeast Arkansans hindered the school's development, Aggie's staff persisted. That success was evident in the enthusiasm with which they entered into the support of the war effort, and even more in the durability and stability that Aggie demonstrated in the 1920s.

Pictured with President Kays (left) is another veteran board member from the early years, Henry M. Cooley, who was active in raising funds to locate the school in Jonesboro and who served as the school's attorney.

CHAPTER II

"REALLY, IT WAS A COW COLLEGE"
The Junior College Era

This bird's-eye view of the campus, captured in 1923 from the top of the Administration Building, includes (from left) the D.T. Rogers residence (registrar), faculty bungalows, Barnhart Hall, the power plant, Lewis Hall, the YMCA building, the engineering building, the beef cattle barn, the swine barn, and the dairy barn. The buildings are located along Aggie Road and Nettleton Road (now Caraway Road).

Yet the period between the war and 1931, when the college granted its first four-year degree, was marked by a sort of business-as-usual atmosphere. Students attended their classes, worked on the farm or in the living facilities, participated in college organizations, and sampled the entertainment offered by downtown Jonesboro. Meanwhile, faculty and administration continued to dedicate themselves to quality education in agriculture, as they had when Aggie was primarily an agricultural high school. They also devoted themselves to the new junior college curriculum, which by 1923 included a full two years of offerings in arts and sciences, pre-medicine, pre-engineering, and education, as well as in agriculture and home economics. Moreover, the college continued to expand its physical plant. Throughout the 1920s, life at Aggie took on the familiar trappings of an agriculturally oriented institution of higher education. After all, as Ottoleine Detrick Echols, a member of the first four-year graduating class, remarked, "Really, it was a cow college."

A decided effort was made to recruit students, and Buddy Kays recalled that his father employed a professional for this task. As Kays said:

❝ He [President Kays] had a fellow on that [recruiting] at all times. In fact, the fellow worked for a couple or three schools at the same time. . . .One week he'd be up here. Another week he'd be for one of the others. ❞

John Miller, who grew up near McCrory, Arkansas, recalled being recruited for Aggie:

❝ My dad was always interested in good schools for the community. He was on the school board down there and worked at it. I don't know why, but he got this idea in his head that I should . . . go to college and learn to be a pharmacist. So a fellow came . . . through that part of the country down there getting students for Aggie out here, and he came down and talked to my dad and talked to me. It was a chance to get to be a pharmacist. . . . He came on out to where we were. Seven miles out in the country. I don't know how he got a line on me. ❞

Sometimes a faculty member would be instrumental in bringing a new student to Aggie. For example, Dean E.L. Whitsitt influenced Clyde Duncan:

❝ I got to know Mr. Whitsitt. I was in the grade school over in Lake City, and I was a charter member of the 4-H Club work. I had exhibited a ten-ear specimen exhibit of corn at the county fair and won first prize in the junior division and then competed for the championship and won top honors for the thing. Somebody gave me a dollar an ear for it—for planting Reed's yellow dint, full pollinated variety. E.L. Whitsitt read that in the *Jonesboro Tribune* or *Sun*, so he wrote me a letter saying that he wanted to come over and see me sometime. He didn't get over there till in the summer. He came out and talked to me about coming to school here. When I got over here, Mr. Whitsitt—well, he sent me some books. He was a great guy to do that if he liked you. He sent me several books on agriculture. ❞

While President Kays actively sought high school and college students, he expanded the physical facilities of the institution. In 1919 construction began on a YMCA building. Financed in large part by private donations, especially from board member Robert E. Lee Wilson, the building was constructed almost entirely through student labor. One function of that building was to provide apartments for the faculty and students. Lillian Eldridge, who arrived

at Aggie in 1923 when her husband took over the newly created position of registrar, recalled the apartment that Mother Warr prepared for them:

❝ She put a great big—two beds looked like hospital beds—great big high beds and a folding chair in one of them [the rooms], and the other two were empty. Over the lavatory in the bedroom there was a mirror that made you look like a Chinese or Japanese. . . . Then the upstairs to this place—to this building—were rooms where students and faculty stayed. One of the things we had to do after we moved in was to look after those students upstairs. ❞

Other building projects in the late teens and early twenties were a new beef cattle barn, built in cooperation with the United States Department of Agriculture and the University of Arkansas Extension Service, and an engineering building. This latter structure, completed in 1923, later served the campus as a fine arts building.

After the students had been recruited and arrived on campus, a substantial amount of their time was taken up with classes. However, when they looked back on those years, former students did not dwell upon the drudgery of attending lectures, preparing homework, studying, and

taking examinations. Instead, they remembered unusual occurrences in the classroom, peculiarities of instructors, or special relationships they might have had with faculty members. For example, Duncan's position as a breakfast waiter in the dining hall afforded him the opportunity to cultivate the good will of an instructor in whose class he was having some problems:

❝ We had a fellow named Nixon who was teaching woodwork. Mr. Nixon, he hated to get up in the morning. . . . I was taking woodwork, and I guess I was the worst student that he ever had in woodworking. I was waiting tables, and Mr. Nixon would come in real late. I'd stick around and wait his table—wait for him. He always liked to have ham and eggs. We had a colored woman who was the cook, Fannie, and she'd say, 'Clyde, now you want to make a good grade in that woodworking course. We'll fix Professor Nixon right up.' So when Mr. Nixon would come in, I'd start to the kitchen and say, 'Same thing?' He'd say, 'Yeah, same thing.' Fannie would have his ham and eggs and toast just right—the right temperature and all—with coffee and orange juice, always orange juice. I'd take it out to Nixon. He'd really enjoy his breakfast. ❞

Duncan's attentions to his instructor paid ample dividends:

❝ It came time to grade, and he'd grade us on what we made in the woodworking course. We had to make a lamp is one thing I remember, and those desks were made so that a student—two shared a desk, and you could put two lamps in one desk. I shared mine with Joe Ridey from over here in Monette. Joe was good in woodworking. He really knew how to make a lamp, anything. I was the world's worst. So Mr. Nixon said, 'This next class period will be final exam, and that will be judging your lamps.' Each student would stand at his desk and wait, and Mr. Nixon would come along. He'd pick the lamp up and look at it and examine it real carefully and write down in his little black book the grade. I knew I was going to flunk that course even though I'd been pretty nice to Mr. Nixon. He came by when he got to me and looked down in that desk, looked down at my old, beat-up lamp and said, 'That ain't your lamp, is it, Clyde?' I kind of stuttered around. He said, 'Here's your lamp.' Then he pulled out Joe's lamp that he'd probably graded the previous class period. He said, 'That's about the best lamp in here.' He gave me a good grade. I didn't say anything. I figured that he knew what he was doing. ❞

21

Student members of the Arkansas National Guard, Battery C, 206th Coast Artillery, Anti-Aircraft, drilled south of the Administration Building under the command of Captain Harry E. Eldridge.

The National Guard unit is shown here at summer camp at Fort Sill, Oklahoma, in 1926. Students in the unit spent two weeks experiencing military life, including reveille, calisthenics, guard duty, guard mount, regimental parade, retreat, review, and inspections of various kinds.

Some time afterward, Duncan, having graduated from Aggie, returned to the campus. His former instructors were praising him for his accomplishments, and "Mr. Nixon was sitting there with a big grin on his face." Someone asked the woodworking teacher, "Clyde Duncan really took care of you, didn't he, Mr. Nixon?" To this Nixon replied, "Yeah, he really took care of me with those ham and eggs. But let me tell you one thing. I took care of Clyde, too."

A course that many students regarded as being particularly difficult was C.M. Hyslop's chemistry class. Ottoleine Echols recalled how she managed to get through her chemistry labs:

66 The first semester, why, he [Hyslop] had us, a girl and a boy, work together as partners. Well, the boys did all the work done, and the girls would do the sitting. So the second semester he put his office in between, and the supply room was in between the two rooms. And the girls had one end of the room for all of their experiments, and the boys had the other. Well, we girls did twelve experiments every Friday afternoon because we had to turn in a sample, and we would each one give the other a couple of samples. And the poor boys would even have to come back on a Saturday in order to keep up. And one of the boys asked, 'Dr. Hyslop, how did the boys get behind?' 'Well, those girls are just smarter than you all.' 99

Miller recounted a prank that students played in one of Hyslop's labs. Hyslop set up his students to do their classroom experiment and then left them on their own. But his inattention backfired:

66 Just above was the botany or zoology lab. There were ventilators from the bottom here up to there, and we were down there generating some kind of gas. I've forgotten what now. [The] professor up there—he had been in the war—and he stuck his head out the window and hollered at us down there. We were making nerve gas. It was pretty potent stuff. He couldn't stand it. We ran him out. 99

By the 1920s a variety of sports activities were available on campus. Competition in track and field began on a rudimentary basis in 1924. By 1930, the school had developed a track team that was undefeated.

Aggie's football team prepares to leave for a game with Ole Miss for the first game of the 1925 season. In spite of the enthusiastic send-off, the team went down to defeat. The Aggies ended the season in a tie for the conference championship.

Fannie Cash (at far right) served meals to Aggie students in the 1920s and later became Senator Hattie Caraway's cook in Washington, D.C.

23

Echols also recalled an amusing incident when her home economics class tried to impress Dean Whitsitt:

" A meal we served was to Dean Whitsitt. . . . And we had, I don't know what the meat dish was, but anyway it was kind of like hash. But they did it a little more fancy than that, and the girl who was supposed to be serving that night—the skillet had a handle, a wooden handle that flipped—and she flipped it all on the floor. And there were wooden floors at that time, so you know how hard it was to pick up. But she managed to get up enough to bring to the table. "

No matter how close faculty and students might be, their relationships retained vestiges of conflict. Students delighted in taking advantage of the foibles of their teachers and in outwitting them, especially in matters of tests and grades. Echols told how she and some co-conspirators befuddled a psychology professor:

" He had us alphabetized in class. And a girl that I finished high school with . . . was in the class. And her name was Derrick, and mine was Detrick, and she went with a boy named Dupwe. Well, that put him on the other side of me, so after . . . [the professor] called the roll, we just quietly swapped seats so she'd be sure to sit by Charlie. And I don't think the poor old soul ever knew the difference. "

Echols also recalled how students in the late 1920s got foreknowledge of examination questions:

24

" One of the professors had a son who . . . had access to the exam questions. . . . And there used to be down at the railroad tracks—there was a little shed down there to catch the . . . train. And that's where we learned what the examination was about. "

But cheating was not always undetected, as Clyde Duncan and a friend discovered in Mary P. Babcock's Latin class:

" I was so involved in student activities, feeding hogs, and one thing or another. Latin wasn't the thing I came to school to major in anyway. So sitting on the back row, I had an old girl right in front of me named Snyder. . . . She was a real brain in this Latin. I'd look over her shoulder . . . and look at her writing paper and all that, you know—trying to get a grade out of that course. I knew she was going to make a good grade. So Miss Babcock asked me something on the back row, so this little Snyder girl whispered. She knew I was having a hard time figuring it out. You can't whisper in a little old classroom without the teacher knowing it. Miss Babcock didn't pay any attention. She just went right on and let Miss Snyder get by with whispering the answer to me. At the end of the semester, she read out these grades. She didn't post them. She read them. Her name was Dee Mae Snyder. . . . Dee Mae should have made an A, see, ordinarily. So she read these grades out. Two or three top students made As, and it came down: 'Dee Mae Snyder and Clyde H. Duncan—C.' She joined us together. "

Babcock, who joined the Aggie faculty in 1921, had a much different effect on Lenita Stack. The Jonesboro native could still visualize the Latin teacher's vivid descriptions of the architectural monuments of ancient Rome. When she traveled to Italy years later, Stack could still hear her old instructor from Aggie describing the Forum, the Coliseum, and other Roman buildings.

Even in the early 1920s labor on the college farm or in the residence halls and dining room was required of all students. Nelson Crum

learned the hard way that such work was not avoided with impunity:

" You had to get up at five o'clock in the morning, go down and feed your mules, and curry them and harness them, and come back and eat your breakfast like a farmer's meal. And then you'd work a half day on the farm for a period. . . . But I didn't have time with the curriculum to take all the subjects that I had to have to graduate and do the farm work, too. So to heck with that mule business. I knew how to handle a mule, anyway. Because I grew up on a farm. And I thought my dad was about as good a farmer as Mr. Kays was and could teach me. So I just backed off of it, but, of course, I couldn't graduate. That year there [were] only three male students eligible to graduate. And the other two flunked, and I didn't do the farm work. "

Duncan performed several jobs at Aggie between 1919 and 1922. He fed hogs, swept out the Administration Building, and carried out other menial tasks. So he viewed a job under Mother Warr as a definite promotion:

" If you made good at janitoring and feeding the hogs and all that, why, you got to work in the dining room. As I said, I started feeding hogs. . . . And then eventually—I was here three years—my last job of working was in the dining room. And Mrs. Warr put me in charge of the faculty table. "

Duncan also put in some time milking the college's prized dairy cows:

" We had a bunch of old test cows, and you had to get up at three o'clock in the morning and milk these cows. I drew that assignment for one semester. . . . I was kind of on second string on milking. I had small hands. We had these four cows. You know dairy cows. They get used to you. They won't respond to anybody but you. I'd go down there and milk these four test cows, and I'd talk to them just like you talk to a person. I'd rub them on the back with an old mop that had disinfectant on it and wash off their udders. Talk to these cows all the time you're milking them,

Fan support begins to take shape by the mid-1920s as evidenced by Sara Stuck, a member of one of the early cheerleading squads.

see. One of them's name was number Old Sixty-Six. They were on state test, and Mr. Kays wanted to win the top honors with this Old Sixty-Six cow. The other three weren't too far behind. There she was going along producing very, very well that semester I was milking her. "

Unfortunately, Duncan became ill and could not continue milking the cow that had become so attached to him. The dairy foreman was sure that nothing could be done to solve the problem caused by the young milker's absence, but Duncan recalled that the resourceful President Kays came up with a solution:

" He said, 'Clyde is small. Just have one of the girls milk those cows.' There were plenty of girls here from the farm. So he goes over there to the dormitory and gets one of those girls. I don't know what the girl's name was—from Ash Flat or somewhere. She was a small girl, and she went up there and started milking these cows. Mr. [H.C.] Cocanower [dairy instructor] told me later

Coach Herbert Schwartz (left) poses with the 1928 "Gorillas." With the increasing emphasis on college work and diverse academic offerings, the athletic teams changed their image by doing away with "Aggie Farmers." In 1925 athletes became the Gorillas, a nickname that lasted until 1930 when they became the Indians. The 1928 football Gorillas finished the season with three wins, three losses, and one tie.

Margaret Wall also had memories of the conflagration:

❝ A student phoned my father . . . early that Sunday night to say that the Administration Building was burning. And Daddy and Mother rushed over, of course, as quickly as they could. We watched from our dining room window. It was early in the morning at the opening of the second semester and very cold. Very little could be done about the fire, and the destruction was complete. There were brick walls left standing, and that was practically all. ❞

Ottoleine Echols saw the glow of the fire from her home in downtown Jonesboro, about two miles away. The building was completely devastated, although quick work by the firefighters saved some of the student records. As Tex Plunkett recalled:

❝ All they saved in the fire was the safe that contained the students' records. They were able to play the fire hose on the safe and keep it cool, and even so some of the records were pretty badly scorched. A few students had to be asked what subjects they had taken and what grades they had made. ❞

Wall recalled that her father, the college bursar, was especially concerned about the records as he watched the building burn: "Daddy wanted to rush in to see if he couldn't get some records from the business office." She confirmed Plunkett's observations about the fate of the records:

❝ The student records and the business records were kept in a large, iron safe, a quite tall safe, and I do remember the big, thick door. And the firemen poured water on that safe throughout the night. When it finally cooled—and I do believe it was about two days later—when it finally cooled and was opened, many papers and records were badly scorched and turned brown, but they were still legible. ❞

Aggie was undaunted by this major loss. In fact, business was conducted as usual the next day. As Wall said:

❝ By eight o'clock Monday morning, the very morning of the fire, temporary offices had been set up in the old mechanical building where agricultural equipment had been stored, and the post office reopened there. Classrooms were parceled out any place a spare room could be found. I remember very distinctly—I was an English major—sitting in one of Dr. F.W.

Plunkett's classes . . . that was held after the fire in the dairy barn and watching weevils crawl in swarms up the walls. The room had been used formerly to store cattle feed, and it wasn't unusual for weevils to be there. ❞

Echols recalled that the students arrived early at the campus that Monday morning, hoping that classes would be dismissed for the day. "But they'd already thought of the cow barn," she lamented, "so I don't think we missed a class."

Both students and faculty lost books and papers as a result of the fire. But fortunately no one was injured, even though, as Buddy Kays reported, the president "had to keep [mathematics professor] Dean Ellis from going in to rescue his equipment." The extent of the damage to the building itself was illustrated by a small detail recalled by Homer McEwen, son of a staff member. Just a child in 1931, McEwen remembered:

❝ We combed through the ruins for days after that when it'd cooled off, and we'd find molten silver that'd come from some of the old trophies, cups that were on display there. ❞

While the loss of this important building was a severe blow to Aggie, plans were immediately put into effect for its replacement, the present R.E. Lee Wilson Hall. The fire demonstrated conclusively the institution's ability to survive and bounce back. It also heralded a new look for the campus, since Wilson Hall established the architectural style that would be developed in most construction over the next several decades.

Another major event at Aggie in 1931 was a happier one, a visit by noted humorist Will Rogers. As part of a fund-raising tour to assist drought victims, Rogers presented a program in the old armory building on February 11, 1931. Buddy Kays enjoyed one joke that Rogers told:

" He pulled a piece of paper out of his pocket and said it was a telegram from the studio: 'Dear Will—If you don't hurry up and get back, you will be amongst the unemployed.' **"**

During the next few years, many Americans were unemployed. And the students who attended Aggie would feel the pinch of the Great Depression. But the institution was looking forward to a period of growth and development that would constitute a major step in its progress toward becoming Arkansas State University.

CHAPTER III

"I COULD NEARER GET A THOUSAND DOLLARS NOW THAN A DOLLAR BACK THEN"
The Depression Decade

Wilson Hall, the successor to the original Administration Building, opened in 1932. Although built at the same location, Wilson faces north, rather than south toward the railroad tracks like its predecessor.

The new administration building was named to recognize the personal and financial contributions of R.E.L. Wilson, a member of the board of trustees from 1917 until his death the year after Wilson Hall opened. His portrait hangs in the lobby of the building.

40

In the decade of 1932-43, Arkansas State experienced the contradictory forces of growth and constriction. Growth was apparent in an increase in student enrollment, in confirmation of four-year college status, and, most obvious of all, in the construction of several impressive buildings. Constriction was equally obvious in the absence of generous state appropriations and the relatively impoverished nature of prospective students and their families. The Great Depression, which began in 1929, reached ever deeper into the savings of Arkansas' families until the crisis began to ease about 1935. However, the effects of this great economic panic continued until the outbreak of World War II.

Under the leadership of President Franklin D. Roosevelt, the federal government attempted to provide higher education with emergency assistance that state governments failed to contribute. Arkansas State College—Aggie received this formal title in 1933, the year Roosevelt took office—was a beneficiary. Several structures that comprise a part of the present physical plant were products of Washington's generosity. What prosperity the campus enjoyed in the 1930s suddenly ended in 1940-41 when the threat of war became a reality. By 1942, the first full year of war for the United States, ASC's grounds were practically barren of young men.

Although Aggie graduated into a four-year institution, one aspect of student life remained unchanged—the necessity for work to earn funds for fees, room, and board. In fact, the stringency of the Depression made labor even more necessary. Edgar Kirk, who attended Arkansas State from 1932 to 1936, recalled the severity of this grind:

66 Work is about all I did when you think of having to go to school, working your way at fourteen cents an hour and carrying the average load. You don't have a whole lot of time for other things. However, that is not as low a wage as it might seem because in those days the fees for a semester at Arkansas State were twenty-five dollars. Board and room was twenty-five dollars per month, and we were all in about the same predicament. The Depression hit about everybody. I was no hero, or I was no person making a great, terrible sacrifice, because I guess you could say that was the standard for those days. That's about what all of us were doing. 99

Among this youthful work force, Mother Warr's waiter boys occupied the most conspicuous place. Margaret Wall, daughter of this hard-working matron of the kitchen, remembered these workers well:

66 The waiter boys wore starched, white, long-sleeved coats of some material, I presume, sort of like duck. They wore trousers and ties. Their hands were always immaculately clean. They would come through the washrooms and wash their hands, of course, before they began waiting the tables, but they would serve the dishes, and then after everybody else had eaten, they would clear the tables, take the dirty dishes back to the kitchen, and then they would sit around the tables themselves to eat. 99

Much more went into the chores in the kitchen than mere table service. Kirk recalled "scrub day" with the most sorrow:

66 I remember so well that every Saturday morning was scrub day. The floor in the cafeteria was concrete, unpainted concrete. So every Saturday morning the chairs had to be placed on top of the tables. We took brushes and soap and water hoses and got in there and scrubbed the concrete floor of the cafeteria, rinsed it off, then wiped all of the chairs, cleaned all the tables, and the tables were heavy oak tables made of boards, and they had cracks between the boards, so scrubbing the tables—that was one of our jobs after doing the floors. I'm sure we wiped a lot into the cracks because almost every Saturday morning we had to take knives and clean the cracks in the tables. 99

The college farm continued to employ most of the student workers. While not so popular or profitable, the income from these grueling chores at least enabled some eager scholars to pay room and board. Marshall Matthews engaged in a multitude of duties for the college:

66 I soon got a job working for the college farm and grounds. The salary was fifteen cents per hour. During my sophomore year I became better known and became a student foreman working about fifty boys. We did what the physical plant does now. Plus, we drove mules furnished by R.E. Lee Wilson. We worked in the hay fields, filled up two large silos with sorghum cane for the dairy, built concrete fence posts, and fenced the farm, dug drainage ditches and what have you. We had security duties at the football games. We were a very busy bunch of hard-working young men. We milked the cows by hand, slaughtered the steers and hogs for the cafeteria, [and] fired the boiler for the heating plant. 99

This task of milking cows was fatiguing, and the boys arrived in morning classes often unable to concentrate on their studies. The milkers worked "from three o'clock in the morning till six and again three hours in the evening," recalled Max Edens. "And some of the boys were unable to even hold a pencil in their hand after milking a cow for three hours in the morning."

Such a regimen of labor gnawed away at study time and constrained the more efficient students to organize their time. Marshall Matthews kept a taxing day:

66 I found out that scheduling your time was absolutely necessary to do the job. . . . . A typical daily schedule at one time was as follows: breakfast at five, farm or campus work until first

class, studying in between classes in room or library, three-thirty in the afternoon to six collecting data for Dr. Brown's research program, seven to eight tutoring in guest room in Danner, eight to ten delivering cleaning and pressing and collecting clothing to go to the cleaners, and then to bed at ten. 〞

One pair of energetic brothers found a unique, but profitable way to earn expense money. Max Edens recalled:

❝ In 1937 a fellow from Memphis down at East Lake one summer taught me how to tie flies out of rooster feathers. So my younger brother and I caught all the roosters around Tyronza, and we tied flies all summer. And we hitchhiked to West Memphis and Blytheville and Jonesboro every Saturday displaying cardboards of these flies at Western Auto stores and drugstores and automobile places. And we made over $500 that summer tying flies. We could do about eight flies an hour for fifty cents apiece: four dollars an hour. That was fabulous money. So I took the $500 and went to college for a whole year. 〞

As the Depression cut more deeply into the economy, President Kays, who had guided the school through much hardship, sought a new source of assistance—the federal government. One national program that offered some promise was the Reconstruction Finance Corporation (RFC). Although President Herbert Hoover had created this office earlier, the RFC became more accessible under his successor, Franklin D. Roosevelt. Roosevelt's own creations soon began to extend a helping hand. The Civilian Conservation Corps (CCC) assisted many students of ASC. Buddy Kays recalled the presence of a CCC camp on Billy Goat Hill (now the Army Reserve Center and Country Club Golf Course):

❝ Now that was not a normal CCC camp. They had boys in there all the way from totally illiterate to college students, and they arranged schedules on the campus here for the boys to take college work and work part-time with the CCC. Student teachers from the campus went over there at night to teach the illiterates. So it was an educational camp, and the buildings were of a better quality than a lot of the camp buildings were. They used the CCC out here on the farm to build ponds and plant the pine trees. 〞

The National Youth Administration (NYA) also provided much-needed educational support for young men and women. Although some NYA participants at Aggie were city boys and unfamiliar with the work at a "cow college," they soon learned. Jasper "Jap" Hunter, who worked for the college farm and maintenance crew for many years, supervised these eager, but often inept young men:

❝ They would go to unharness a mule. Instead of unbuckling the collar and taking it off of the mule's neck, they most invariably would try to slip the collar off over the mule's head. Usually when this happened, the mule would become excited, and the student would wind up with a lost mule. 〞

Some of the more fortunate youths financed portions of their expenses through private loans. Of course, the banks seldom incurred the risks of student loans. Edgar Kirk sought out a neighborhood "banker" in the summer of 1936. As his senior year approached that fall, he had earned enough for all of his expenses except tuition—fifty dollars. Kirk's father suggested that he approach a neighbor, John Cole, for a loan:

❝ Now John had the reputation for being the wealthiest man in the whole neighborhood and almost in the county. He dressed like a tramp. He lived in a hut that was literally propped up to keep it from falling off the supports . . . propped with two poles to keep it from sliding down the hillside. A two-room building, and it had two outside doors and no door between the two rooms. You had to go out on the ground from one room to get into the other room. . . . John was sitting in what we called a cane-bottom chair up in the chimney corner, leaned back in the corner with a magazine in his lap, and as I approached and spoke to him, we started a little conversation. 〞

Neighbor Cole proved to be rather superstitious as Kirk remembered the encounter:

The National Guard unit musters for inspection in this 1937 photograph. Mobilization of the unit in 1941 decimated enrollment on the ASC campus.

The graduating class of 1934 included the first two Wilson Award Winners, L.W. "Tex" Plunkett and Violet Ruth Fox. The award, established by R.E.L. Wilson's family after his death in 1933, recognizes the outstanding graduating students.

Faculty families such as the Daniel F. Pasmores often resided in apartments on campus. Dr. Pasmore established the foreign language department in 1930, and his wife headed the art department. The campus became the playground for their children.

66 He wanted to tell me about his magazine. It was a book of astrology that . . . he had heard about on the radio and had ordered, and he said he followed that book religiously. . . . A few days before he had read in his book a warning for that day that he must beware that somebody would try to beat him out of some money that day. He said, 'I hadn't been in the field plowing an hour when two men came to the field and wanted to borrow a hundred dollars apiece. I just wouldn't let them have it.' Well, of course, I wondered what the thing had for today. But I talked on, and by the way, as he sat there, protruding from his right overall pocket was the butt of a 38, I believe it was, revolver. . . . All of this made my asking for the money even more difficult. 99

But, Kirk recalled, he was now ready to get down to business:

66 Eventually, I picked up courage to say, 'Mr. Cole, I'm wanting to go back to college for my senior year. I have a job to pay all of my way except for my fees which will amount to fifty dollars for the two semesters. I don't have any money and no way to get it, and I'm wondering if you would loan me fifty dollars.' Before I had much more than got it out of my mouth, he said, 'Sakes alive, sakes alive, yes! Will that be enough?' I was sure that his reading of the predictions of the astrologist for that day had not been too bad. But I then asked him, because I had heard that if he lent anybody money that he

In addition to "thumbing" rides, ASC students could ride the city bus from Jonesboro to Wilson Hall for five cents. Automobiles were scarce, and the 1932 catalog noted that, while they may be essential to attendance for some students, they were at the same time detrimental to scholarship.

tied them so securely that they could hardly breathe—I then asked him, 'Mr. Cole, what kind of security are you going to demand?' He said, 'Your dad will sign a note with you, won't he?' I said, 'He certainly will.' He said, 'That's all the security that I wanted. Tried to help my boy get an education—he wouldn't take it. Neighbor over here, Martin, tried to get his boy an education and he wouldn't take it. Glad to do anything I can to help a boy who's trying to get an education.' **"**

A few down-on-their-luck students found sources of borrowing on campus. President Kays supported some young people with personal loans. Lyle Bettis, later a brother-in-law of Max Edens, borrowed $300 from this willing administrator. Edens (the source for this story) added that Bettis hoped to repay this note by working part-time in the school barn. However, said Edens, Bettis "never did milk enough cows to pay the interest on his money." Linual Cameron, another struggling collegian, reluctantly concluded that he had no alternative but to withdraw from classes:

" I came over here hoping to get a job to go to school. Well, along in November I ran out of money. And a dollar back then was like—well, I could nearer get a thousand dollars now than a dollar back then. So, I went in to see Cap Eldridge about withdrawing from school and to see if I could get part of my fees back, and Cap Eldridge said, 'What are you going to do?' And I said, 'Quit school.' And he said, 'Why are you quitting school? . . . You can't quit with this much of the semester by.' I said, 'You can if you don't have the money.' He said, 'I'll let you have some money.' He handed me fifteen dollars. I finished the semester on fifteen dollars. **"**

While these eager young scholars contended with the niggardly economy of the 1930s, ASC enjoyed a surprising spurt of growth. In a decade of human want, the physical plant of the campus mushroomed. Beginning in 1932, with the completion of Wilson Hall (the replacement of the burned-out Administration Building), several new structures dotted the grounds. Two new dormitories, the old science building (now the

College of Business) with attached drill hall, and a power plant followed in quick succession. President Kays constructed these buildings with federal funds, which the government made available through its many work-relief programs. Franklin D. Roosevelt called his administration the "New Deal," and that name certainly fit the consequences of these monies for Arkansas State College. The resourceful Kays tapped this financial wellspring with the assistance of Senator Hattie Caraway, a resident of Jonesboro and strong supporter of ASC. With Reconstruction Finance Corporation (RFC) funds, Kays erected two dormitories—Danner Hall and Women's Residence Hall (later renamed Caraway Hall). Buddy Kays noted that "there was quite a to-do to get that funding," since the bureaucrats offered conflicting advice:

" At one time one of them told him just straight out that the RFC wasn't set up for small loans. It was set up for the big loans, and that's all it was set up for. Amongst other people working in the RFC, there were Harvey Couch, who had been head of the Arkansas Power and Light, and the man above him was Atlee Pomerene. Now Atlee Pomerene had been senator from Ohio and also the special prosecutor in the Teapot Dome scandal. Well, the connection there was this—one of his relatives was married to my aunt. . . . But, nevertheless, one trip up there, Daddy was having trouble with the bureaucracy. He went to see Atlee Pomerene, and when he heard about the run-around that was happening, the order went down to cut out the run-around. That's when Couch asked Daddy why in the heck he didn't let him know that he knew somebody up there. **"**

Many people intervened on behalf of Arkansas State in the negotiations with the RFC officials. Judge Archer Wheatley, a state representative at that time, helped to obtain the consent of the state government to receive federal aid.

As many buildings went up during the 1930s the opportunity for accidents was always present. Two fatalities occurred, one of the victims being Guy Davis, a seventeen-year-old and president of his freshman class in 1936. Buddy Kays recalled these tragic events:

❝ A good deal of the power plant down here which is not part of the ag set-up was built with student labor. There was one death on that job. One boy fell over the edge of a scaffold one day and hit the slab with his head. Wilson Hall had one fatality. That one was—they had built a hoist on the south side of the building (they had one on the north side, and they were putting in an extra one), and they didn't guy as they went up. One man was climbing the outside. The other was coming up the inside to attach the guy wires, and a puff of wind came along and tilted it. The one on the outside jumped clear. Of course, he was in the hospital for a period. But the other one was crushed. He died several hours later. ❞

Among the new buildings, the replacement for the old Administration Building occupied the most prominent place. The very conspicuousness of this structure in the heart of the campus meant that naming it would be important. Tex Plunkett had a firsthand view of controversy surrounding the search for a name. The board of trustees had this responsibility. Plunkett recalled:

❝ After Wilson Hall was completed, Mr. Cooley, who was a lawyer uptown, an excellent lawyer, had been on the board a long time. He wanted the building named after him so badly, he hurt. So one board meeting he came to the meeting early. Mr. Banks always got there early with his revolver. So Mr. Cooley was a little man and bald headed. . . . And he said, 'I think this building ought to be named Banks Hall.' Of course, he expected Mr. Banks to say, 'No, Cooley.' Mr. Banks looked at him with piercing blue eyes—looked at him and said, 'Mr. Cooley, you don't have any money, and I don't have any money, but Mr. R.E. Lee Wilson has a lot of money. And there's a lot of sidewalks that needs to be built and trees need to be planted, and landscaping needs to be done, so I think we better name it Wilson Hall.' Mr. Wilson hadn't showed up yet, of course. He had farther to come than anybody else. So they kicked it around, and Mr. Wilson came in, and Mr. Banks said, 'Mr. Wilson, we have named this building

The Commons Building, containing a dining hall, dormitory rooms, and infirmary, was dedicated in 1937. The ASC Board of Trustees attended the dedication ceremonies. Construction of the building was the talk of the town because it was built from the top down to save clean-up chores. The building later became State Hall and then the College of Nursing and Health Professions.

Wilson Hall. It's got a little proviso on it. You are going to have to finish the grounds and plant some trees.' And some of the elm trees that you see on the campus today were planted then. So Mr. Wilson lived up to his agreement. He sent [mule] teams and men over here and graded the grounds and planted the trees, and they built sidewalks and that sort of thing. Now that's how Wilson Hall got its name. 🙶

The expansion of the asphalt road network and the growth in numbers of automobiles encouraged more students to attend the institution in the 1930s. Lloyd Langford, son of a local funeral director, described the various ways that he and his friends made their way to school—a far cry from the slow and cumbrous wagon transportation of a decade earlier:

🙶 Aggie Road . . . was a main way to go. You could go down old Nettleton Road or Nettleton Avenue. You went to the intersection at what is now Caraway and Nettleton, and on the left there was a restaurant-type operation called Park-Er Inn. It was a hang-out for a lot of the college students. Turning north at Caraway Road and Nettleton Avenue, you crossed both railroad tracks to get into Arkansas State as you do today. One of the railroad tracks there accommodated another mode of transportation . . . called the Bull Moose. It was a part of the Jonesboro, Lake City, and Eastern Railroad. The Bull Moose as such was powered by diesel, I believe it was, and it usually pulled one or two cars, depending on the time of the year. You could ride from the J, LC, and E depot, which was on Johnson and Main Street in Jonesboro—you could ride from there out to Arkansas State. They had a little lean-to built out there, in case it was raining or snowing. 🙶

Other means of transportation were available. At the cost of five cents, students could ride a city bus. This motor transport made regular stops in front of Wilson Hall and other places before the lumbering vehicle made its way to downtown Jonesboro. Many students hitchhiked. To "thumb a ride" became a common part of student lingo. Homer McEwen used his thumb frequently:

🙶 We would hitchhike from about the same place as the bus stopped or maybe on down in front of Williams Service Station going toward town. Then coming back, we usually walked from the movie or wherever we'd been down to the corner of Church and Cate where Hollingsworth Dry Cleaners used to be. And we'd hitchhike from there. And the townspeople were very good about picking us up. Later on it was regarded as a little bit of a dangerous thing to do, I suppose, to pick up hitchhikers, but the people of Jonesboro were very good about picking up students and taking them to and fro if they were going that way anyway. 🙶

Lloyd Langford, one of the few fortunate persons to drive the family car to college, often picked up his classmates along the road:

🙶 We had an old four-cylinder Dodge that I was allowed to drive. My brother and my sister

This early music group, directed by Guy French, performed at football and basketball games in the early 1930s and was one of the first groups to perform on the new Wilson Hall stage.

46

and a next-door neighbor—the four of us rode out. By the time we got there the car was full, maybe four or five in the back and as many as we could stack in the front, because somebody was out there thumbing a ride to Arkansas State. When we came to Jonesboro from school, it was the same way. 🙾

The accessibility of Jonesboro and other nearby areas to the Aggie students opened new possibilities of entertainment off the campus. Joyce Lichtenberger McEwen recalled the joys of Park-Er Inn at the corner of Nettleton and Caraway roads. This establishment was the nearest off-campus sanctuary for the residents of Arkansas State:

🙾 We used to dance all the way from Commons Building down to the old Park-Er Inn—just dance on the road. We didn't have any trouble with cars at that time. Park-Er Inn was a real nice restaurant. . . . It was a barbecue place operated by Roy Garrett. Marvelous food. And it was just in a grove of trees, but it was a popular hang-out for the kids. 🙾

Downtown Jonesboro still remained the most alluring place for the students. Marshall Matthews made many trips to Main Street to enjoy a movie or some good food. There were, however, certain enticements along the way that Arkansas State College did not endorse:

🙾 We would hitch a ride to town on Saturday night or walk as there were very few cars on campus during those years. Many would go down Aggie and cut across town to the theater or Prince's Cafe, which was a good place to congregate. We cut around the red-light district. Remember those were the early thirties before prohibition was repealed. Times were hard. Corn whiskey was sold from under the bar rather than from behind the bar. Many road houses were about Jonesboro. A typical one was Joy Land on Nettleton Avenue. There was a bar and dance hall, beetle organs for music, girls to entertain, and dice and poker games in the back rooms and cabins in the rear. Fortunately, few college students had time to care to frequent these places. A circus was held just west of the ROTC

Some important people on campus included (clockwise from top left) Frank W. Plunkett, Ashley Robey, Homer E. McEwen Sr., and Lucille "Mother" Warr.

47

building each year and a carnival down Aggie Road. This was adequate, along with the Strand Theater and the Bloody Bucket. Danner and Women's Residence halls and lounge rooms were recreation halls for playing and dancing. 🙙

Although President Kays and his supporters had crusaded against the red-light district, the demi-world remained a resilient form of entertainment for some persons. Marshall Matthews and his friends concluded that the prostitutes were an allurement that they could do without. He recalled:

🙛 We didn't have time to do a lot of things like that. . . . Most college kids then . . . had a hard way in those Depression years. . . . The reason we would cut across town to keep from going through the red-light district was because the women would bother you when you went downtown. They would open the door and let their little dog run out, and he would nip at your leg and give them an excuse to come out and talk to you and during the conversation open the robe that was real loosely attached and then invite you in. Most college students didn't care for that stuff. 🙙

Although students found ways to escape the campus for brief periods, most of them spent the majority of their time within the confines of the college grounds. Regulations continued to circumscribe their conduct. Matthews remembered:

🙛 There were no posters or bulletins on walls or doors. Smoking was done outside classroom buildings. Blue jeans were thought of as work clothes by many and not clothes to be worn to class. If a letter was worn on a jacket or sweater, it was a big A or ASC. If you stayed in jail overnight, you knew that you were dismissed from school. No hearing was held. 🙙

Warren W. Nedrow, who served as a faculty member and assistant dean of men in the thirties, confirmed this stern code of discipline. As the supervisor of the College Club building (he and his wife resided there), Nedrow obediently enforced the rules:

🙛 The students were not allowed to have radios in their rooms. Of course there was no television then. Every now and then I would confiscate one [radio]. By the time school was over in the spring I'd have an office full of radios, and I'd give them back to the students. 🙙

Any event that brought boy and girl together was closely observed by college officialdom. William Wyatt, a journalism major and member of the print shop staff, desired to escort his girlfriend (the future Mary Grace Wyatt) to a nearby circus on Aggie Road. "We had to take Miss Bernice Livengood, who was in charge of the dormitory, with us," he recollected. Tex Plunkett had some vivid memories of courting customs in that era. The center of wooing was Barnhart Hall, the women's dormitory:

🙛 Barnhart was about where the one side of Reng Center is, and Lewis was on the other end with a walk between them and a crosswalk that went down to the main building which became Wilson Hall. The boys could walk the girls from the cafeteria as far as the crosswalk, and then they had to stop. There was a redbud bush there that was known as the 'burning bush,' and that's where the boys had to leave the girls. The girls had to go their way, and the boys had to go back to their dormitory. 🙙

The benevolent paternalism of President Kays' administration probably weighed more heavily upon the female members of the collegiate community. Joyce McEwen resided in the newer dormitory, the Women's Residence Hall, and endured a very tight code of regulations:

🙛 I had a single room that had a single bed and a dresser and one little study table and a straight-backed chair. No carpets, no floor lamps. You furnished your own lamp. And we had dorm monitors who were usually pretty good-size girls who saw that we kept hours. We had to be in the dormitory by seven o'clock each night unless we made the Honor Roll. And then I think we were allowed to stay out until about nine-thirty or ten on week nights. But on weekends I think we could stay out a little later. I really can't remember exactly what the hours were. But I do know that everything was very, very strict. We weren't allowed to keep food in the dormitory. 🙙

Each week of the academic year, the moral authority of the college came to bear directly

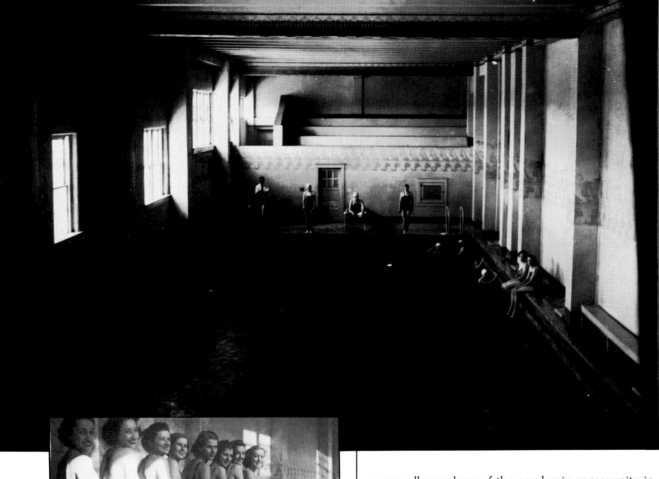

Arkansas State boasted the first indoor swimming pool in northeast Arkansas—complete with bathing beauties. These photographs were taken in the late 1930s.

upon all members of the academic community in a gathering called "chapel." This campus conclave served several purposes: religious and moral instruction, entertainment, and announcements (in an era of relatively unsophisticated media). Lillian Eldridge, a history teacher in the training school, sat through many of these weekly sessions. Dean E.L. Whitsitt often presided, although he might resort to fillers to take up the time:

66 We were there thirty to forty-five minutes, an hour, or something. After they had a prayer, Bible reading, a song or two, usually they'd have maybe somebody to talk or something. Whatever the business of the day. We couldn't leave until the bell would ring. So Dean Whitsitt was master of ceremonies. Always, he had charge of the chapel program, and ofttimes he'd have to fill in to stay there till the bell would ring. He had a little story he told every morning. It was about a little bird that sat on a fence, and that little bird sat there and sat there and sat there. That little bird was a pretty little bird and just sat there. About the time the bell would ring, he'd say, 'Sat there till all his tail feathers fell out.' Of course, everybody knew what was coming because it was told every day. 99

The classroom remained the primary focus of activity at Arkansas State. Most classroom time was routine with few out-of-the-ordinary incidents to remember. Of course, the instructors guarded this sanctuary of learning jealously and resented any unnecessary interruptions. Mildred Vance, a student from Sedgwick, Arkansas, generally earned a reputation for devotion to studies and always obeyed the strict code of classroom decorum—with one exception. She enjoyed upsetting Bernice Livengood, instructor in English and history. Vance related:

66 Chewing gum irritated her, and each day I would make a special effort to put gum in my mouth so I could chew it in front, and to this day, I do not—I do not know what motivated me to do that kind of thing, and she would make such an issue of it. And she'd say, 'O.K., Mildred, spit your gum out so we can start the class.' And so I got where I could hit the wastepaper basket from quite a long distance, you know. And I never did tell my parents about that. 99

Vance studiously avoided troublemaking generally; others of her classmates were not so conscientious. On one occasion, one of her youthful colleagues caused her some discomfort and embarrassment in Wendell Davis' French class:

" We were taking a test, and this basketball player was sitting beside me, and we were on a front row right by the desk, and Mr. Davis was sitting up there. . . . I got most of mine worked out on the French exam—this fellow just reached over, took my paper, and copied everything that I had written on it, and there I was with no paper—nothing! And I kept holding my head down and flipping my pencil, and I was really angry about it, and finally the fellow gave me back my paper, and I finished it up. He got an A out of French, and I think I got a B. "

Pranks continued to provide a much-needed release of pent-up energies. The upperclassmen looked forward to hazing new freshmen. Sometimes, this practice went to excess, as Marshall Matthews recalled:

" One time we took the freshmen and left their clothing in the basement of a small dormitory on campus, Lewis Hall. Put them on a truck and hauled them out into the country about four o'clock in the morning in the nude and turned them loose out there. We let them come back on campus, still in the nude, and we sat on campus and watched these white streaks go from hedgebush to rosebush and finally into the basement of Lewis Hall to get their clothing. Later in my college career, the seniors—some of the more mature students—would see things that they didn't appreciate, so they thought that hazing was something that shouldn't be carried to this extreme. "

Tex Plunkett, an ingenious leader of the pranksters in the 1930s, remembered that he and his cohorts endangered several buildings in one of their light-hearted moods. The students customarily held a pep rally before a game and concluded this gathering with a big bonfire. One of Tex's friends, Von Mullins, was miffed at the coach, who had ejected him from the squad. Tex and the boys decided to ease this grudge by setting fire to the huge pile of kindling and other combustibles a night in advance of the rally. Plunkett narrated:

" We got a hold of all the cans we could get a hold of and filled them with gasoline and dumped it on that pile they had and threw a match to it, and, by gosh, it made an awful light, and we jumped into the car and got away, and we drove down Caraway Road and on into town, and we looked from town to the school, and it looked like, from the light in the sky, that we had set the whole blooming campus on fire. We got worried and decided we better come out. We knew the journalism building was there and the education building, just where the journalism parking lot is now. Just as we got back to Lewis Hall, somebody hollered, 'Fire,' and the students began to pour out. One of the lads—I think it was Gene Higgenbotham—had a tea kettle that had gasoline in it. He was going to throw it on the fire, but he was afraid to and still had it in his hand. Mr. Hart came out of the dorm and said, 'Get some water, get some water,' and Gene handed him the tea kettle and said, 'Here's some.' It was rather a dangerous thing to do. The next day they had a special faculty meeting, and the head cheerleader got up and said whoever'd done that was an 'all-American skunk,' and they were going to have another one the next day. At that time, what they call Baptist College—over in the old high school building that the tornado destroyed—they got all the blame for it. They thought it was some of the Baptist College students sneaking out there setting it on fire. For a long time there, when they were going to have a bonfire, they would have the freshman college students guard it every night. "

Of all structures on campus, the water tower offered these masters of the practical joke the most attraction. Not only was it the tallest and most conspicuous object, but in the words of Edgar Kirk, the tower was "strictly off-limits to us boys":

" It used to stand, as I recall, about 130 feet high in front of Danner Hall almost where the health center is, I believe, now. It had a ladder. It went, of course, all the way up to the platform around the tank. . . . So one night about four or five boys decided that they were going to climb the ladder to the water tower, and they got almost to the tank when the night watchman [came by], who was Vic Lassiter. He carried a big five-cell flashlight, a spotlight. He could throw a

Local fraternities and sororities paved the way for later affiliation with national organizations. The local Delta Omega Sigma was the forerunner of Beta Psi Chapter of Tau Kappa Epsilon.

beam I don't know how many hundred feet. So when making his rounds I suppose he glanced up toward the starlit heavens, and he saw silhouetted up there a bunch of boys on the ladder of the water tank. So he threw his beam of light on them and ordered them down. He carried a scratch pad with him, so as they came off of the ladder, he checked them one by one asking them their name and writing it down as they gave it. The last boy off of the ladder was Kunkel Vance, and when Kunkel came down to him, [Vic asked] 'What's your name?' And he said, 'Kunkel Vance.' Vic challenged him: 'Don't believe that's your name.' He thought he was giving him a fictitious name. The truth of the matter was that he was the only boy in the bunch that gave him the correct name. **"**

As might be expected, Tex Plunkett and his clownish aggregation inflicted the most memorable joke upon this mute object. In 1934 they decided to memorialize their graduating class on the water tank. Plunkett stated:

" In my junior year I was elected president of the senior class. In those days being elected president of the senior class was the same as being elected president of the Student Government Association because the seniors ran everything. I was pretty proud of myself and my friends, too. . . . We decided we would go up there [on the water tank] and paint our class number on it—"Class of '34." We got us a bucket of paint and a brush, and one night we started up there, but the wind was blowing pretty high, and the going was pretty good until right where the tank started—the ladder went up it—you felt like you were hanging out in space. When we hit that part, we felt that was too much, and so we gave that up. **"**

These mischief-makers soon screwed up their courage for another try. Plunkett continued:

" One night when the wind wasn't blowing so much, we decided we'd do it. So I got up there and got up on the catwalk. Lyman Barger, he was the smallest of us. He was a cheerleader at the time. I remember Lyman Barger, Gene Higgenbotham, and Von Mullins. Anyway, we

painted that '34 on there. Lyman Barger did a good job painting a great big 34 and said, 'How's that?' I said, 'Put in the apostrophe for the 19,' and he put a slash for the 19. We were really proud of our work, but we went on to class, and about nine-thirty the order came around that all male English majors report to the president's office. There wasn't more than six male English majors in the whole school. So Mr. Kays let us sweat it out outside the office awhile and finally called us in. The other two boys didn't know what it was about, but we four knew exactly what it was all about. Mr. Kays had grey piercing eyes and looked us all over real good, and he said 'Now, boys, I want you to help me.' Then he made a long spiel about what a penalty it was to deface state property and just scared the gizzard out of all four of us. So he told us that he wanted us to help catch the guys who did it, and we said we would do our best. **"**

Many years later, Plunkett asked the president if he had ever learned the names of the pranksters. Kays replied that he knew the names of the guilty parties the day after the event because "it was written all over us." But to have expelled them would have ruined his enrollment, he informed Plunkett.

The establishment of a print shop also facilitated the growth of a spirit of community. A small newspaper, *The Herald*, became the means of spreading the word. Tex Plunkett, who was nearly as omnipresent as President Kays in the 1930s, played a part in this pioneer journalistic undertaking:

" When I was a student, I was advertising manager and business manager of *The Herald*, and *The Herald* was printed downtown by a town printer. And he printed it whenever he got time to [do] it. Lots of times he didn't have time to print it until it was maybe two weeks past due. So, one day Mr. Kays met me on campus and said, 'Tex, when is the paper coming out?' and I said, 'Mr. Kays, I don't have the faintest idea. That man down there has a lot of work to do, and by the time the paper comes out it will be ancient history.' And then I said, 'I think if I was as smart as you are, I'd find some way to get this paper printed here on this campus somewhere.'

And I don't know if that had anything to do with it or whether he had been thinking about it, but the next year we had a little print shop and film room. It was back in about 1932 or 33—somewhere in there. And since then, *The Herald* has been always printed on campus. **"**

William Wyatt, a student and printer, worked in the print shop for many years. He recalled printing a very special edition of *The Herald:*

" We celebrated the 25th anniversary [of the school] soon after we started the print shop. We had a special edition of the paper for it. . . . We had an old flatbed press there that we ran them off on and did the work on it, and as I said, we printed a little yearbook, 1934, in the print shop, just a small one and then we printed the annual starting in '37-'38. They worked them up, and we printed them and sent them off and had them bound. Soon after that they started getting wealthy enough to have them done otherwise. **"**

Classes in printing soon became a popular part of the curriculum. But to become a full-fledged member of the printers' fraternity, the newly arrived students—the novices—were constrained to endure a peculiar form of hazing. Buddy Kays loitered around the print shop many times as a boy and observed the initiation of the printers' devils:

" First thing they did was teach them the case. The way they did that was they'd take all the typesetting cases and dump them right out into the middle of the table and pi the type. There was all different styles, sizes, and so on. They had to clean the cases out—get them clean—and then re-sort all the type and clean it. By the time they got through with that project they knew the case. Another one was when they were proofing the type. They'd have all these type slugs, and they'd bring them over and show them how to kill lice. They'd pour gasoline and water in there, and while they were looking at it, they'd pull all that stuff together right quick and just spray them in the face. So there's always something going on in a print shop. **"**

In addition to the printing program, Arkansas State College began to offer several new career

The lounge of the new Women's Residence Hall, completed in 1934, was a favorite gathering place for students. In 1961, the dormitory was renamed for Senator Hattie W. Caraway.

courses. A Reserve Officer Training Corps (ROTC) appeared in 1936. The opportunity to earn the rank of second lieutenant in the United States Army attracted many young Arkansans, although the first two years were mandatory for all male classmen. Elmer Mayes, a student and later an instructor in mathematics at Arkansas State, thrived on ROTC. He and his friends enjoyed attending the military classes because of the "fringe benefit" of wearing uniforms on the days they had class in the armory. Apparently, Mayes and others enjoyed the prestige of the uniform. The Army greens or khakis impressed the coeds. Mayes even wore his uniform to Saturday class. Eventually, Colonel W.E. Corkill, professor of military science and tactics, "had to pass a rule to restrict us," said Mayes.

Other benefits flowed from ROTC training. Max Edens learned much about military life and discipline that served him well as a Marine in World War II, especially in the use of weaponry. He also recalled that "we learned to say, 'Yes, sir,' and 'No, sir,' and to march." He and his fellow cadets also "had to be spic and span at all times." To fail in this or any other part of military practices, "you had some demerits to work off."

In a related area, ASC began an aviation training program in 1939. Although not a military undertaking, flight training added some incentive to enrollment at Aggie. The college began construction of the hangar building (now the maintenance department) with Works Progress Administration (WPA) support in the next year. Several runways were projected for the two-year program. Elmer Mayes took flight training elsewhere, but he observed some of his friends learning to fly at the old hangar:

❝ You notice on the east side of that [hangar] the bay windows. . . . Now, there's a purpose of them . . . that was for control, and the landing field was out there where . . . those dormitories are . . . and the trailers and all that. . . . Spud Clark and a few other close friends learned to fly planes out there, and it was practically an old cow pasture. . . . It was quite crude. ❞

As Arkansas State continued to grow in the Depression era, the campus began to develop

Dormitory "bull sessions," including this gathering over homemade ice cream, relieved the routine of classes and campus work. Kneeling is Tin Boo Yee, one of the first international students to attend ASC.

traditions that remain a part of the academic community to this day. These traditions are vital and help to provide a sense of purpose for participants in the life of an institution of higher education. Memorable personalities among the faculty occupy a prominent place in this repository of experiences. Many persons remembered Ashley Robey with great fondness. He demanded high performance in his chemistry classes. Elmer Mayes experienced a rude awakening when he entered the professor's bastion. "Boy, I knew all about chemistry," he recalled. But the arrogance of the entering freshman soon turned to despair. "I was in trouble and happy to earn a C."

The demanding chemistry professor stood out among his fellow instructors. Said Mayes:

❝ Dr. Robey was a very colorful [person]—he wasn't too tall and extremely huge and round. I guess he probably weighed 350 pounds, and he chewed tobacco. And [on] the top floor of the old science building now there was a large chemistry lecture hall. . . .When the class was over, he'd go to that window and raise it and 'Fwoom!!!!' there'd go that amber [tobacco juice]—I don't know how he could talk, but it didn't interfere with his lecture at all. ❞

The portly professor impressed everyone who encountered him. Marshall Matthews, who

ASC's primary purpose was academic progress. The 1930s brought a more modern appearance to classroom and laboratory facilities with the opening of Wilson Hall and other new academic buildings.

was known for his academic excellence, paid Robey especially high praise:

❝ He was the finest instructor I guess that I've ever had. One of the five [best], anyway. He weighed about 315 [pounds], could dance all night, shoes were about a size 7, small feet for a big man. When he played baseball or softball, he was catcher, and when he caught the ball behind the plate if he couldn't reach it handily, he would just bounce like a pepper shaker falling over. He was quite a guy. ❞

Edgar Kirk observed that "everybody liked" Robey, even though students were sometimes hard pressed to keep up with the swift-paced professor:

❝ He could climb the stairs with that 320 pounds in Wilson Hall to the fourth floor where the chemistry labs were in those days. He could climb those stairs more rapidly than any of his students. I've seen him go across the campus. He lived in the College Club, which was over near where the school of nursing is now. I've seen him go from Wilson Hall across campus. Maybe some student would be going along with him wanting to talk to him, and the student would have to trot two or three steps, had to slow down and pick up again to keep up with Robey bouncing that 320 pounds across the campus. He wore work shoes. He had the brogan type as we sometimes called them. I suppose his weight—they gave him support. I don't mean that he was eccentric. He was one of the most popular persons I've ever seen on the faculty. ❞

In spite of the restrictions of weight, Robey maintained a very active schedule. Homer McEwen recalled that this hefty man "would participate in the initiation of pledges" into honorary societies. "If he slapped you on the back," recalled McEwen, "you knew it!" Naturally, Tex Plunkett saw the humorous side of this engaging man:

❝ Best natured fellow you ever saw. . . . At the science building he had to go in the door sideways. . . . He lived in the Kays Foundation, and he never put the car in the garage, because if he put the car in the garage, he couldn't get out of the car. ❞

The student body could never anticipate this rotund chemistry professor. There were no limits to his inventiveness. Lloyd Langford was startled by Robey one cold and icy day:

❝ One morning I went to school early because we had a snow, and on top of the snow we had a drizzle of rain which froze and made ice. . . . I pulled up beside the hill out there in front of [Wilson Hall] and parked. I started in the building. I looked back over toward the old dormitory building. I believe they called it the . . . College Club building, where the instructors and their wives and families lived. They had apartments there. Here came a big round bundle of enjoyment with a stocking cap and a muffler around his neck coming down the hill on a pair of ice skates. I thought, ' Well, when he gets to the bottom, he's going to be in trouble because he's not going to be able to stop. ' But he did. He managed it fine. He just came scooting right on off that hill. I was standing there marveling that a man his size could skate on ice. ❞

A companion dorm for men, practically identical to the new women's dorm, also was completed in 1934. It was named for W.S. Danner, a member of the board of trustees from 1913 until his death in 1933. Danner was a planter and gin operator in Crittenden County and a former state senator.

Perhaps one of the best known members of the faculty in the 1930s was F.W. Plunkett, professor of English and father of Tex. In many ways, he was the opposite of Ashley Robey. Joyce McEwen remembered the elder Plunkett as "something else":

66 I will never forget one time in class in Shakespeare he wanted to emphasize a point. You know, he was really a very, very small man. He hopped onto his chair and then hopped up onto his desk. And he shook his finger at us. And he just quoted Shakespeare on and on. I don't remember what he said but I remember his doing that. 99

Students quickly observed that Plunkett possessed eccentric habits. Elmer Mayes remembered that Plunkett came to class one day without his tie:

66 And when he realized that, he grabs his coat—shirt collar—and said, 'Excuse me! I came to class undressed!' He went back to his office and got his tie and put it on and came back. 99

If this man of letters suddenly developed an itch on his left ear, recalled Mayes, "he took his right hand over his head and he scratched his left ear." Strangely, he scratched his right ear "like all normal people would" with his right hand.

This diminutive professor did not strike all students the same way. Mildred Vance enjoyed some of his classes, but concluded that Plunkett harbored some resentment toward female students:

66 I always had a feeling he didn't particularly care for the female sex. I don't know whether that was just my opinion or not. I recall being kind of afraid of him, not in a . . . personal sense, but he was very demanding. . . . He would say things to the female students. He said one thing I recall, that female students should not be allowed to go to college. That their place was in the home. And you know, he did receive his doctor's degree from the University of Virginia, and I believe at that time it was an all male school. He felt very strongly that women had no place in being here. And our themes were

severely criticized in terms that you really had to be correct, not only the uses of your language, but the way you spelled, and because he really made a mountain out of a molehill. I recall that the word 'all right'—I spelled it one time, A-L-R-I-G-H-T. I still see students spell it that way. Never again would I ever do that because this was an example that [he] used. . . . Later I had several courses with him. I took Victorian poetry with him, and I loved that course. . . . He really was a scholar. And once you got past this feeling, 'Well, I'm a female, and he doesn't like females,' then you could really enjoy him and appreciate him. 99

The crusty English professor possessed a keen interest in his students, as Edgar Kirk learned upon graduation:

66 Doc Plunkett took me for my first interview to get a job when I was to leave here with my brand new B.S.E. degree. On the trip over and back he talked . . . [about] experiences of his early days of teaching in the one-room school and how he got out and sought jobs and maybe [would] get one and then ride horseback all over the country looking for a better one. . . . He gave me some of his philosophy of education, and one little statement that he made I have thought of so many times. He said, 'Kirk, after all my years of teaching, and all that I have heard about methods and how to teach, I've about decided that it doesn't make a whole lot of difference what method that you use.' He said, 'I've decided that the poor student will be a poor student under any teacher, and the good student will learn in spite of the teacher.' I've thought about Doc's statement dozens of times in my teaching career. 99

This learned scholar suffered from the malady that most people mistakenly associate with academics—absent-mindedness. Buddy Kays recalled that "along about five o'clock in the afternoon you'd see Mrs. Plunkett going over to the office to pick him up because he'd forget to come home!"

The faculty of Arkansas State labored under a common handicap of the small college in the 1930s—a heavy teaching load. This burden of

classes generally prevented the academics from research and publication. However, one of Aggie's most respected teachers—Mary Watters—transcended this drawback and published scholarly books. Her publications were probably the first serious works of this faculty and a worthy example for her successors to follow. Edgar Kirk reported:

66 When I came over here, I came as a math major, and I did well in math—enjoyed it, but my sophomore year somehow I staggered into a history class, and that class was taught by one of the most able professors that I have yet encountered, a woman, Dr. Mary Watters. Her interest was in Hispanic American history. She did her dissertation, I believe, on the history of the church in Venezuela and was one of the best lecturers I've had in graduate school or anywhere else. She got me interested in history, and I switched majors. 99

The publication of a book was a difficult undertaking for any faculty member in the Depression era. Margaret Wall, who graduated in the first four-year class, assisted Watters in the preparation of her manuscript, a biography of Simon Bolivar, the South American "George Washington" and liberator in the wars against the Spanish Empire. She recalled that Watters was a brilliant teacher:

66 She was writing a book on Simon Bolivar, and I typed that book for her in the evenings to help her and to make some money. Typed it by the page, and it was a very exciting experience. I was working part-time as I did when I went to college. I would work under Daddy's [C.V. Warr's] supervision, and I worked in the administrative offices. She had a typewriter. I believe it was a portable. I'm not sure, but it was difficult to get all those footnotes in there, but we made it. Then she later wrote another book but maybe after she left Arkansas State. 99

Although not a member of the faculty, Senator Hattie W. Caraway became a much-beloved benefactor of Arkansas State College. When her husband, Senator Thaddeus H. Caraway, suddenly died in 1931, his wife filled

56

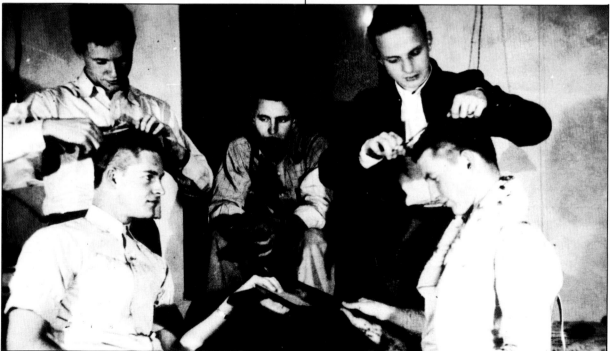

Diversions at ASC took many forms during the 1930s. Relaxing in the Wigwam, altering appearances to conform with the latest fads, necking, and picnicking were activities that were easily affordable during this Depression decade.

The entire student body, faculty, and board of trustees pose in front of the old armory (present museum area) in this late 1930s photograph. Identifications available include (front row, from left) (1) Harry E. "Cap" Eldridge, (2) Dean B. Ellis, (4) Henry W. Hollard, (5) Donald F. Showalter, (6) Bernice Livengood, (9) Lillian Eldridge, (11) Eleanor Heuver, (12) Nannie Rogers, (13) Clyde McMeans, (14) F.W. Plunkett, (15) Daniel F. Pasmore, (19) W.L. Mack, (21) V.C. Kays.

out his unexpired term and then won re-election. President V.C. Kays was so indebted to her for help in obtaining federal funds for building projects that he awarded her the honorary doctor of laws degree. Caraway Road is named for this family. Many former students of ASC remembered Hattie Caraway, not for her assistance to the college, but for her personal charm. Mary Grace Wyatt played in her bridge circle:

66 Oh, yes, she was a lovely somebody. . . . Usually she would shuffle three times and she just said that repeatedly, 'Once or thrice, but never twice.' She was a good bridge player but very kind. Now some of the faculty wives were not that kind. I never played for blood myself. I could appreciate her for that because she was—it didn't matter how big your mistakes, she always had something nice to say to you. 99

President Kays continued to impose his personality upon Arkansas State College after many years at the helm. He was ever present and just as likely to appear in a remote corner of the campus as to be in his office. This restlessness perhaps helped to create the public image of this man that persists to this day. Tex Plunkett recalled Kays' daily routine:

66 He spent about three hours a day being president, and the rest of the time he was out on the campus putting in a sewer line or a water line or doing some kind of work. He usually got . . . to his office in the morning at seven-thirty and stayed until about nine o'clock, and then he came back to his office about three o'clock, looked through his mail. Then at five o'clock he went home. After he got home, he and his wife and son usually went to the picture show. That was almost routine—every day practically. At least they went to a picture show every time they showed a change. 99

Margaret Wall, who became Kays' personal secretary, noted similar qualities—a penchant for activity and a searching mind:

66 Mr. Kays was a man who wanted to be out and on the job. He did not want to be sitting at

that desk. He was a very active person. He was very interested in obtaining buildings. At that time it was necessary to get a physical plant going, an adequate one, and so he concentrated a great deal on that. And he would be out. If they were building at the armory, he was going to be down there supervising or maybe helping pour the concrete. He would come in, and he'd have splotches of concrete and wet sand on his shoes and on his suit. That didn't matter. It was all right with him. He was not one to sit in his office. If he had something to do, he stayed there and did it, but he was out all over this place, on the farm, at the dairy, over at the dining hall, checking on dormitories, checking on some concrete or some sidewalks or whatever. 99

Those who worked closely with Kays soon held him in awe. He seemed to possess intuitive knowledge and an uncanny power to predict the future. Cap Eldridge noted this characteristic:

66 He was a brilliant man. Outside of one general in the Army that I served under, he's one of the smartest men I've ever known. He could tell you what you were going to do next year. You wouldn't believe it, and you'd do it. It's the funniest thing I've ever seen. He just had that insight into humanity. He knew what people were going to do. He'd tell me what was going to happen six months to a year in advance. I'd make notes of it, and then I'd bring the notes back to him. 99

This perceptive college executive was always available to his students, and he often took a personal interest in their welfare. Not only did he extend personal loans to needy members of the student body, but he intervened with faculty and staff on behalf of the young scholars. Mildred Vance remained very grateful for the president's intercession:

66 After the first six weeks I wasn't doing very well. But remember I was a very young student, and I recall that he asked me to come into his office, and he asked me why I wasn't doing very well, and I said, 'Well, I didn't seem like I had enough time, and I wasn't sure that I knew how to switch from one course to the other.' And he

Students from varied backgrounds were a visible part of the academic community.

looked at the number of hours that they had me enrolled in, and he called in someone, and I don't recall who it was. I rather believe it was the dean. I think it was Dean Whitsitt. And they had a rather serious conversation in front of me, and . . . I dropped two courses, and then I carried 18 hours. **"**

The task of maintaining Arkansas State College on a minimal budget in a time of nationwide Depression demanded much resourcefulness and shrewdness. On one occasion, when the state failed to appropriate money for faculty salaries, this energetic man negotiated credit with local grocers. Although the college apparently avoided a repeat of this embarrassment, such a possibility lurked in the background for many years. Warren W. Nedrow was surprised upon his arrival in 1936 when someone apprised him of the institution's financial stringencies: "When we first got there, people said, 'Now establish credit at a grocery store because some months you might not get paid.'"

This ability to find a way out of such dilemmas enabled Kays to hold the college together when lesser men would have given up. He possessed the instincts of a "horse trader," a quality not out of character in rural Arkansas. Fred Barnett, a student in one of the first classes at Aggie and later an automobile dealer in Jonesboro, ran afoul of this "horse trading" ability and came out second best:

" When I was in the Chevrolet business here, why, he wanted a bus. He said, 'Fred, I don't have anything but seven mules to trade you.' I said, 'I don't know what to do with mules, Mr. Kays.' He says, 'Well, I'll tell you what. I'll give you seven mules for a bus.' Well, he talked me into it. He gave me seven mules, and they were so old they couldn't stoop to get water. I was traveling quite a bit then, and I went down here to Earle and told a man, 'I have some mules I'd like for you to look at.' He was a big farmer. He says, 'Well, if they're any count, I'll buy them from you, Mr. Barnett.' He said, 'Fred, they can't stoop to drink water they're so darned old.' I gave those mules away to a fellow down here that would take them off my hands. **"**

This devoted college leader was such an ever-present part of the campus community that his absence was noticed immediately. Cap Eldridge, the registrar and "second in command" to V.C. Kays, was shocked in 1936 to learn that the president would be absent for an entire year:

" I was so-called acting president. . . . Mr. Kays and the board came in one day and . . . said to me, 'Mr. Kays has got to go to the Federal Land Bank for a year, and you're going to run the institution.' That's the only instructions I ever got. **"**

Such services as this endeared Eldridge to the community and helped to foster the growth of a saying current in this region in the 1930s. When a young person decided to attend Arkansas State College, an observer would respond: "You're going to V.C. Kays' and Cap Eldridge's college?" Eldridge could never understand this, because, he always maintained, "I didn't have any more to do with it than they did. I just worked there."

The accomplishments of the 1930s were achieved with only a modestly sized staff and very little equipment. Tex Plunkett recalled that, with the exception of the president, the registrar, and perhaps the dean of the college, administrators did not have the services of a secretary. To be a member of this small clerical staff under President Kays could be taxing. He kept everyone busy, as Margaret Wall well remembered:

" I would go into Mr. Kays' office and take dictation, and then I'd come out to transcribe, and if somebody came to the counter and wanted to pay board, I wrote a receipt for the board. I was not the only one. Anyone who worked in the office, that was the situation. Of course, I was his secretary, and that was my main responsibility. Then, if there was some reason Daddy couldn't be down to put up the mail, I would go down to put up the mail in the afternoon, rarely ever in the morning because it was a much larger job then. I would go down and sell stamps or postcards or rent a box to

The ROTC Cadet Corps, established in 1936, parades beneath the watchful eye of Major William E. Corkill, professor of military science.

some student or someone down at the post office. Everybody did everything, and we worked long, and we worked hard. We often worked at night. During the time when we were applying for and trying to get those loans through for the Reconstruction Finance Corporation for the dormitories, I worked many a Sunday afternoon. I worked on Thanksgiving Day. Just anytime there was an urgency about something, we came and worked, all of us. The post office was opened for a short time every Sunday morning. There was no closing on Saturday or even Sunday. **"**

As a student during this era, Joyce McEwen noted the absence of secretaries and office equipment. "The teachers did their own typing," she said. "They usually furnished their own typewriters, too, which were old, old manuals." Only the very highest officials were privileged to have a telephone. Homer McEwen recollected that those elite few were the president, dean of the college, business manager, and registrar. Not even department heads possessed this rapid means of communication, although pay telephones were normally placed on each floor of the most important buildings.

President Kays insisted upon exceptional frugality in vacation periods. Warren W. Nedrow, head of the department of biology, recalled that the faculty and staff did not receive vacations with pay in the thirties. In order to maintain a steady income, employees had to work the Christmas holidays and any other period between semesters. Nedrow still has a copy of his report, "How I will keep busy on November 28 and 29," which was presented to the administration to confirm his presence in his office in an off-period. This work schedule was aggravated, according to Nedrow, by the absence of heat in offices during the holidays:

" All the heat was turned off in buildings, but you were supposed to work, and so I'd run a long tube from a gas pipe in a laboratory into my office and hook it up to a bunsen burner. **"**

It is apparent that much of the hustle and bustle on campus in this productive era of the college's history occurred in and around President Kays' office. He infused much energy into his subordinates. To work on Sunday was not uncommon, even in a region that regarded this as a day of rest. Perhaps Mildred Vance best

characterized this remarkable man and the academic community that he created:

" I think the university belonged to President Kays. He built it partially through his own effort, and he saw most of the faculty and students as his children. But he saw them as a part of his family or a part of his work force. And sometimes he would differentiate. But frequently in his administration, you know, teachers would have to clock in, and they had to clock out in the afternoon. . . . And there was no leaving the campus during the day. And if you left you had to get permission. And so in that sense, I'd say that he played the father figure role. As you know, it was his school, and everyone that came here . . . became a part of his family—I think he had a very personal interest in what everybody was doing. **"**

Even this dynamic man was answerable to higher authority—the board of trustees—although these superiors possessed absolute confidence in V.C. Kays in the 1930s. While the members of the early board were a conscientious and active group, they were a part of a rather rough-hewn, even lusty age that seems distant today. Tex

Plunkett often attended sessions of the board as a secretary and publicity officer:

“ Every morning at seven-thirty I reported to Mr. Kays' office while he opened his mail. If he found anything in his mail, or if he had thought about anything, then he told me this would make a pretty good publicity story. As he got better acquainted with me and felt that I was rather proficient, oftentimes he would ask me to the board meeting. So this is my first experience at a board meeting. Mr. Banks—W.L. Banks—he was chairman of the board. Then there was Maurice Block. He was from Paragould. Then Mr. Wilson of Wilson, Arkansas, Mr. Cooley of Jonesboro, and either Miss Pearl Davis or Mr. Whitaker. But I think Miss Davis came on later. I think my first board meeting was all men. . . . Mr. Kays was in his office gathering stuff together. I was kind of sitting over in the corner out of the way where he told me to sit. They were sitting around the table. Pretty soon Mr. Kays came in and said, ‘Mr. Banks, I think we are ready to start.' Mr. Banks reached down and pulled out a revolver and rapped order and said, ‘The meeting will now come to order.' I tell you what, I was a mighty good boy at every board meeting I attended from then on. That absolutely seems impossible today, but I will swear on a Bible that it happened. ”

This free-wheeling style of the board of trustees could hardly be maintained today. W.L. Banks presided over meetings with a firm hand, and intruders were frowned upon. Tex Plunkett observed one such gathering:

“ One of my friends that I played tennis with a great deal was editor and publisher of the old *Jonesboro Tribune*. He decided to attend one of the board meetings. Evidently, the board didn't particularly care for his being there. He just barged in anyway. Mr. Banks said, ‘Mr. Murray, you're not welcomed here.' [Donald] Murray gave him a little back talk. Mr. Banks picked up his revolver and said, ‘Mr. Murray, I said you weren't welcomed here,' and Mr. Murray left the room. Later I contacted Mr. Murray on the tennis courts and he said, ‘You know, I believe that guy would have shot me.' I said, ‘Why for?' he said,

‘I don't know, but he's had the reputation of already killing a couple of men.' I said, ‘Were they newspapermen?' He said, ‘I don't know, but I'm not going to be the first one.' ”

This behavior should not cloud the fact that W.L. Banks devoted many years of service to Arkansas State College. Buddy Kays recalled:

“ Mr. Banks was on the original board of trustees, and he was there for about thirty-seven years or better. He was one of the last of his kind probably. The old term, ‘Southern gentleman,' would apply to him. He was a pioneer in a lot of respects. I don't believe he ever did buy a developed farm. He always started with a fresh one and developed it. He went broke a few times, but he always came back. ”

The new library on the ground floor of Wilson Hall included study tables and reading rooms. The Wigwam and post office also were on the ground floor.

One of the prominent features of the campus in the 1930s was the new football stadium at Kays Field. This massive new concrete stadium—it could seat 5,000 spectators—was calculated to attract the sporting audience of northeast Arkansas.

Even before the stadium was completed, townspeople were being attracted to the campus through a variety of events. Cleveland Kohonke, a resident of nearby Nettleton and later a student, recalled:

66 My brother was staying in the old dormitory here, and it was nothing for my mother and I and some others to walk from Nettleton up here. And we walked up here and saw plays and different things put on in the Administration Building. 99

Although many years were to elapse before the athletic program would grow into independent status on the campus, varsity sports began to attract a following well before World War II. While the campus possessed a new concrete stadium, the security arrangements lacked something in the 1930s. In the absence of a fence, President Kays dragooned students and employees into guard service. They literally formed a wall of human flesh around the field in order to prevent interloping. But such an emergency measure could not prevent eager, but poor spectators from getting a look at the game. Elmer Mayes and his friends found a way:

66 I'd stand over here . . . where the old dredge ditch is—just stand along the banks of that and watch the football games, and then after they'd open the gates [at halftime], we'd go around and go in the game. 99

Spectators often crowned the adjacent railroad dump as well as a small knoll where the Dean B. Ellis Library and new communications-education building now stand.

While the Aggie football team was a spirited aggregation in this period, its won-loss records sometimes left something to be desired. As Tex Plunkett explained, what the Indians lacked in size, they made up for in imagination:

66 The Indians would keep driving and never could get to the goal line. Anyway that train would come through there every so often during football practice and during the game. Anyway the Indians were on the ten-yard line and fourth down and no field goal kicker. And the train let out a loud blast, and [to distract] one of the boys said, 'Oh, my Lord, they've had a train wreck,' and they snapped the ball, and the ballcarrier walked across the goal line. Now if that was true or not, I don't know. It was before my day, but that's one they told. 99

The halftime entertainment was always something to look forward to, although the college did not yet support a marching band. Other forms of celebration were readily available. Marshall Matthews remembered these events at homecoming:

66 Some of the halftime entertainment . . . was letting freshman boys catch a greased pig or climb the flag pole. Homecoming was a very big day, beautiful queens and court, elaborate floats and all. I was president of the Engineering Club one year. Our float won a trophy. It was a ship of state with light posts, portholes, smoke coming from the two stacks. The float was powered by a Plymouth car completely hidden underneath. The smoke from the stacks was generated from the back seat of the auto. 99

As the world moved closer to war in the late 1930s, a growing sense of foreboding reached the campus. When President Roosevelt stepped up peacetime mobilization in 1940-41, the pressures of this process soon afflicted ASC. Enrollment went into sharp decline and classrooms became practically empty. Only a few students remained—young men whom the military rejected and females whom the government had not yet decided to summon to duty. One reason for this sudden decline in enrollment was the presence of the National Guard unit on campus. Battery C, 206th Coast Artillery, an anti-aircraft formation, was activated in early 1941 and eventually shipped to Alaska.

Elmer Mayes and Cleveland Kohonke were among the student members of Battery C. Mayes, who spent five years in service, recalled:

66 I guess at the time that we were mobilized on January 6, 1941, we . . . made up—well, more than half of the battery—us college students. When we were mobilized, that interrupted my college education here. 99

The buildup emptied the classrooms of most young men, but the vacant educational buildings were not so obvious to the public. Perhaps the abrupt decline of the athletic program best dramatized to the public the disastrous effects of the wartime mobilization. The desperate coaches resorted to physically unfit students to fill out the decimated athletic squads. Elmer Mayes remembered the effects on the basketball team:

66 I recall that they got national publicity the season . . . after us leaving. . . . They played the University of Kentucky, and it's quite common now for a hundred points to be scored, but Kentucky beat the Indians, oh, something like 120 to 60 or something of that nature. Got a write-up. One of my friends that was not an athlete. . . . One leg was quite a number of inches shorter than the other . . . had a strong body, and he filled in there, and he was on that team. 99

This exodus of healthy males into the armed forces injured football just as severely. Cancellation of games would have cost the college what was as scarce as healthy males—money. So the show went on, as Tex Plunkett recalled:

66 The Guard was pulled out. . . . We didn't have anybody to play but crippled and little bitty boys. If we didn't finish the schedule, we had to forfeit the money, the guarantee, and we went ahead and played it even though we got beat terribly bad by everybody. I don't think we won a single game. A story [circulated] about one little back we had, where he was going to carry a ball out of the end zone, and they put him on the one-yard line and just carried him and the ball back into the end zone and the official called a touchdown for the other side. I was mad. 99

As ASC's young men marched off to war in the early 1940s, their departure ended an era in the history of the college. Although the wartime emergency interrupted the routine of educating the youth of northeastern Arkansas, there was little doubt about the permanence of the institution. This was not the case a decade earlier. In the early 1930s, the abject condition of the state treasury persuaded a group of prominent persons to seriously propose the abandonment of Arkansas State College and its three Act 100 counterparts, all created in 1909. Only the resourcefulness and dedication of V.C. Kays—with the invaluable support of R.E. Lee Wilson and others—prevented this grim event. But by 1943, a generation of east Arkansans had grown up with the college, and the possibility of such an educational loss was unthinkable.

After a decade of major effort, ASC's campus took on the look of a college. This aerial view was taken about 1940.

CHAPTER IV

"THEY WERE VERY DIFFICULT TO SET ABSOLUTES FOR"
An Interval of Instability

V.C. Kays served as the school's first president from 1909 to 1943. Through his leadership, the State Agricultural School became the First District A&M College in 1925 and Arkansas State College in 1933.

The dramatic decline in the student body that began at the outset of World War II continued throughout the conflict. The first loss of students occurred when the local National Guard unit was activated in January 1941. By September of that year the number of students at ASC had fallen twenty percent below the figure for the same date in 1940. After war was declared in December 1941, many students began to feel the pressure of the draft. Others volunteered for the armed forces. By September 1942 enrollment had declined another twenty percent; only 329 full-time students were attending Arkansas State College. The trend persisted throughout the war years, though increased enrollments began to be evident as soon as hostilities ceased in 1945. Joyce McEwen, whose academic career was interrupted by government service during the war, graduated from ASC in 1946. McEwen compared her class to the previous year's:

❝ There were fifty-three seniors when I graduated—twenty men and thirty-three women. And, of course, that was really good. The year before there had been forty women and only eight men. ❞

During World War II, the campus hosted several military training schools. Both the college and the community had to adjust to the needs of transient soldiers who were soon shipped to combat areas in Europe or in the South Pacific. Arkansas State College also had to accommodate the inmates of a German prisoner of war camp

set up on the site of the former CCC camp, about half a mile south of Wilson Hall. After the war, faculty and administrators faced additional problems: the paucity of supplies and funds, together with a sudden influx of students, many of whom as veterans presented special kinds of difficulties. In spite of this instability, by 1950 campus life was beginning to return to normal. Developments pointed toward the expansion of ASC, which would be the dominant theme of the institution's life in the next two decades.

The first unit to arrive on campus during World War II was the Army Administration School, established at ASC partly through the office of Senator Hattie W. Caraway. In April 1943, a detachment of Army Air Cadets arrived. It was followed in December of the same year by a unit of the Army Specialized Training program in basic engineering. This military presence had both positive and negative effects. Tex Plunkett praised the military trainees as lifesavers for the college:

❝ The school was in terrible, terrible shape because we had employees, and nobody had much to do. And that's when Mr. Kays worked out some plan with the government to have the air crew cadets sent here. ❞

He recalled the cadets' first reaction to the ASC campus:

❝ The first unit came from Fort Breckenridge, which was a camp fort near St. Louis. And when they came in, they came in on a train and got off down on Caraway Road, and it turned out it was a very foggy morning. And all they could see were those old barracks buildings where the prisoners of war had been [the former CCC camp], and they thought they were going to be there. The officers that were unloading them didn't know where they were supposed to go either. But, anyway, the train moved out, and they marched them in this direction. And they couldn't see any of the university at all, but when they got up to where it is now the fine arts and journalism building, this group of boys saw the steam tunnels and burst into song. And they were relieved because you can imagine what shape they were in—colds and such—after living in tents. ❞

The military also created added burdens for the college staff, especially those who were charged with seeing after living arrangements for the trainees. According to Margaret Wall:

❝ The dormitories and all available rooms were crowded with enlisted men in their khakis on the campus for a few weeks before a special train would pull up at the spur down here, and they would load on that train and another group would come in. ❞

The kitchen and dining hall had to submit to a military regimen, which Mother Warr dreaded. Her daughter related:

❝ The kitchen was always clean and sanitary. It was immaculate. They worked at it all the time to keep things clean and sanitary, but it was different with the Army. And she felt that one colonel just tried to be difficult in his inspections. He would rub a white-gloved hand over the bottom of a cooking pan. She did have some acute health problems during these months, but she never gave up. ❞

These regularly assigned units were not the only military burden for the heavily taxed kitchen staff. Lula Nedrow, who took over the kitchen after Mother Warr fell ill, recalled that many troop trains stopped for meals. The food service maintained three eight-hour shifts to serve these and the resident hungry mouths. According to Nedrow:

❝ Often at night the government would be moving troops, and usually that would happen around three or four o'clock in the morning—before daylight. . . . They would march up to the cafeteria where we had breakfast ready for them. And I was the only one that ever knew that that train was coming in. The colonels would tell me . . . and I was only allowed to tell the people that were going to prepare the meal about an hour ahead of time before all those people came in. ❞

The kitchen staff could not predict the appearance of these special trains, although as many as two a week was not uncommon. An

Horace Thompson (right), a 1925 Aggie graduate, served as the college's president from 1943 to 1945, followed by W.J. Edens (left) from 1946 to 1951.

atmosphere of mystery always surrounded these events. "As soon as they ate the meal," added Nedrow, "they'd march them [the soldiers] back to the train, and they'd be gone before daylight."

Even the plumbing in the residence halls had to be adapted to fit the requirements of the "invasion" of the military. As Jap Hunter, longtime member of ASC's physical plant staff, noted:

❝ We got in a group of soldiers that were training for the Air Force. This consisted of about 2,000 soldiers. Well, no way did this university have bathroom facilities and stuff to take care of this many soldiers, so we began to install extra plumbing. . . . We would just take a room, put our plumbing on the floor, build us a platform over the top of it, and mount our fixtures on that. ❞

Occasionally the soldiers had difficulty adjusting to the demands of Army life, or of life in northeast Arkansas. Many of them came to the campus from backgrounds far removed from the rural atmosphere of Arkansas State College. For example, Hunter recalled the soldiers' penchant for gambling:

❝ You've heard the story how soldiers like to shoot craps. Well, I've seen dollar bills piled a foot high even in hard times with a crap game. They'd come in off a hard day's work, they'd throw a table up against a column, and they'd start shooting craps just for amusement. Those that couldn't get around the table would take side bets. 🔊

J.A. "Ike" Tomlinson, who served as dean of men during this period, remembered a more serious problem involving a group of Air Force trainees from the Lower East Side of New York City:

🔊 We finally turned them over to the MPs. They had to shake them down about every night, this sort of thing. . . . They got into it among themselves stealing and knifing, and they wouldn't eat one day. So they [the authorities] would just shut them off, two whole days. They all ate the third day. 🔊

However, Tomlinson suggested, the experience at ASC had a positive effect on them: "At the end of twelve weeks they stepped out on the field in review, and the general was out there. Looked pretty sharp out there."

The German prisoners of war, housed on "Billy Goat Hill" near the corner of present Matthews and Caraway streets, were assigned to various work details in the northeast Arkansas region, including jobs on the college campus. Although the POWs were accompanied by an armed guard, their overseer for the project to which they were assigned was someone on the college staff. For instance, Jap Hunter used the German prisoners to complete several projects including the extension of Dean Street northwards to what was then Arkansas Highway 1. The work could be dangerous:

🔊 I was blowing up some stumps with dynamite. And I tried to keep the prisoners away from the stumps, but I was using [an] electric detonator with wires, and when I'd blow a stump, I'd just pull my wires to me, and I'd go off to another place and blow another stump. But these prisoners were curious to see how deep of a hole that we'd blow. So they'd run up and look in the hole, and they'd smell smoke. Well, of course . . .

anybody that has ever been around dynamite that has had a dynamite headache knows what kind of headache these boys had the next morning. They were crying. You didn't have any trouble after that keeping them away once they found out what kind of headache they'd have. We did a lot of work with those prisoners. 🔊

Ike Tomlinson also had occasion to use prisoner labor:

🔊 I was assigned nine of them to take care of the football field and line it off. They were very fine men, and I don't recall any problems with anybody. Well, I do. One morning we had some assigned to the physical plant over here. They always assembled them over here where the post office is now. Then we came and took our men and went to our assignment with them. Mr. [Ralph] Waddell had a new tractor, and he was looking for a tractor driver, and we were democratic, and we let them volunteer. They all volunteered, and they all wanted to drive it. They got into a fracas among themselves, and we had to separate them. And the commandant up at the camp came and locked them up for a couple of days for creating a disturbance down here. 🔊

In general, Tomlinson thought that the German prisoners were quite well-behaved: "They were very courteous to our students, and if a girl'd go by, there was no whistling or anything of that kind."

Between the Army trainees and the prisoners of war, the Arkansas State campus was kept busy during the war. In fact, as Hunter asserted, the presence of these two groups "helped put this college on the way to recovery." Abruptly after the war, though, the number of students on campus shot upward. But the campus was not really ready for them. During the war years significant construction had languished. Existing structures had often been refurbished to meet the needs of the military. Tomlinson described the physical education building, formerly the National Guard Armory, as he first saw it in 1943:

🔊 When I looked in there, nineteenth of December, the physical training officer's office

was in the front, and on the back—back by the swimming pool—was [a] little dressing room. That's where my commanding officer, Lieutenant Lee, had his headquarters and dressing room. And I was assigned a locker in there. In the drill hall part, which we later used for the gymnasium, right out in the middle of the floor was a tank, training tank, and at this end there were three or four Army trucks parked in there. At the far end there were boxes piled twenty feet in the air—GI boxes painted in GI paint. I don't know what they had in them—kind of a storage area. Probably two hundred pigeons. That was the gym. 🔊

The building was still in poor condition when Robert Moore came to ASC in 1949 to set up an extension program. He remembered the gymnasium floor especially:

🔊 It had a cement floor in it, covered by a black-top floor. That thing would sweat, and they'd try to play ball on it, and the student would scoot around, and his feet slip out from under him. 🔊

Even after money was raised to lay a wooden floor over the concrete, the situation did not improve. According to Moore:

🔊 They put that floor in there, and about the first time it got real wet and sweaty, that floor rose up about two or three feet. They tied it down, they thought, but not tight enough. 🔊

The presence of large numbers of servicemen brought vitality to the campus during the bleak years of World War II. The school housed several military training schools on campus including a unit of the Army Administration School, a detachment of the Army Air Cadets (pictured), and a unit of the Army Specialized Training Program in engineering.

German prisoners of war, posing with campus and community workers, were housed on Billy Goat Hill near ASC and participated in work details on campus.

Tomlinson recalled other evidence of the military presence on campus in the late 1940s—in many cases of great benefit. Surplus military equipment helped the campus meet the needs of the quickly growing student body. "I don't know how we would have operated after the war," he said, without the supplies that were purchased at Army surplus sales. Chairs, desks, window shades, notebook paper, typewriters, filing cabinets, pencil sharpeners, books, and shelving were among the items acquired for the academic programs. For the physical education and athletic programs, Tomlinson was able to purchase wrestling mats, volleyballs, footballs, basketballs, gym shoes, and gym clothes from Army surplus.

Arkansas State needed these supplies, and more. For the immediate post-war years witnessed rapid growth of the student body. That growth was fueled significantly by veterans returning to college or beginning higher education for the first time under the GI Bill. The impact of that legislation upon higher education was well described by W.L. Smith, an education professor and later head of the audiovisual department:

66 It was making available college education to many people who probably never dreamed of going to college previous to that. So I'd say that was an important landmark in federal aid to education. **99**

Ike Tomlinson noted the impact of the returning soldiers, many of whom had matured far beyond their years as a result of their war experiences:

66 The enrollment shot up very rapidly. We had trailers [for families] pulled in all over the place. People living in conditions that were not quite conducive to college-level health, I would say. Money was free among the GIs. Attitudes were quite different from a normal college student, which you might have been used to. We had people, Marines with as much as forty-eight months of field service in Tarawa, places like that I'd never heard of. They were very difficult to set absolutes for. They came back, most of them, with the attitude, 'I'll do what you say, but don't tell me to do it and don't put me in a line.' Which was one of the things that we learned very early on the campus that we didn't ask them to line up for anything. Well, they simply refused to do it. I could understand that. They wanted to be treated as equals. I would say this. I was in charge of some dorms then, and I never had a better group of men for policing the dorm and quiet hours and this sort of thing. They were older and responsible people and knew why they came, and the ones that didn't—they took care of that more than we did. In fact, I had people come and say, 'We asked so and so to move out. We're here to study, and he didn't want to.' So it pretty well ironed itself out. Then we began getting the civilian students back, and I felt one of the most difficult problems was the meshing of the two groups, particularly in housing because shooting firecrackers in the halls at three in the morning didn't go over too well [with] . . . battle veterans—they went out the window or under the bed when that firecracker went off. **"**

These ex-servicemen perhaps received some unnecessary criticism when they arrived at Arkansas State. Warren W. Nedrow recalled that many persons concluded beforehand that these veterans would refuse to study. In his words, these critics would say, "Boy, those fellows are going to come in here and just loaf and draw their pay." The former GIs soon disspelled such cynical notions. "It turned out that those veterans were the best students we ever had," said Nedrow proudly.

Robert Ferralasco, later professor of business education, was one of those veterans who attended Arkansas State in the post-war period. He recalled how he and several of his friends in New Jersey—all in search of a college—decided to attend Arkansas State College:

" Harold [Linderberry] had been in the Air Corps in World War II. He had been an air cadet down here taking his preflight training. He fell in love with Arkansas State, lived in Danner Hall, and talked about what a wonderful place it was. He had decided quite some time ago that if he survived the war, he would continue his college education in Jonesboro, Arkansas. Well, you can imagine the reaction from the three [other ex-soldiers] . . . when we heard Harold talking about Arkansas State. None of us had ever been in Arkansas, much less in Jonesboro. The pictures of Arkansas were the typical ones that would come to your mind with [comedian] Bob Burns and his bazooka, and the slow train through Arkansas, black people out in the cotton fields picking cotton stooped over. We just laughed and joked about that. **"**

But the more young Linderberry talked about ASC, the more he convinced his friends that it was the place for them. So four war veterans from New Jersey made the long train trip south and west. When they arrived in Jonesboro, they were in for some surprises. Ferralasco continued his story:

" Naturally, being from New Jersey and spending quite a bit of time in taverns tasting beer and other things, we were quite interested in what might be available in Arkansas and in Jonesboro. We had heard so many weird tales. Well, Linderberry had assured us that while he had been an air cadet living in Danner Hall that it was very easy without a car to walk down to the bottom of the hill where there was a little beer joint and sit there and drink beer. So we knew then that even though we didn't have a car, we would have ready access to the little tavern at the bottom of the hill. I felt a lot better about it, too, because as we were driving—though it was getting rather dark—you could still see some buildings, and we passed several 'gins' on the way in. I thought to myself how nice if we couldn't get beer, there was apparently a lot of gin available. **"**

Even the discovery that Craighead County had become "dry" did not daunt the veterans. Nor did their first encounter with one of the most frightening experiences that one can have living in northeast Arkansas—a tornado. Ferralasco recounted his first tornado, which occurred while he was living in Danner Hall:

" I was on the top floor of Danner Hall in a single room, the top floor being the fourth floor. And, so help me, the building was swaying. I decided to get out of bed to see what was going on. I thought probably it was an earthquake. I couldn't open my door because of the suction that had been created by whatever elements had been involved outside that night. . . . I'd get my door opened just a little bit, and it would be sucked closed. Finally, I heard someone slamming windows, and apparently they closed the windows in the hall. . . . I ran out into the hall. Some of the more experienced folks around storms of this kind yelled, 'Everyone to the basement.' I didn't ask any questions. I ran to the basement in my pajamas. **"**

Many of the veterans brought psychological scars of war with them. Often their problems in readjusting to civilian life and in coping with memories of battle affected their behavior on campus. Lou Couch, who with her husband

The training school, established in the 1920s, flourished in the 1940s. It served as a laboratory for the college's teacher education program. In the right background is Mrs. Bessie Howell, first kindergarten teacher and director until the training school was phased out.

supervised one of the men's dormitories, spoke of the plight of one young veteran:

66 He went in [to the Marines] under a false age—sixteen. I think he was a big boy. And he would get so he couldn't sleep. He would just get out and run and run and run and run to wear himself out. . . . Then he would come back and sleep. 99

This was not the only case of mental disturbance that she encountered while living in the dorm:

66 We had several cases when they would get sick and—thought they were sick . . . just emotionally . . . upset. And we'd call a doctor for them—to satisfy them. But they couldn't find anything wrong. 99

Many of the veterans used alcoholic beverages to deal with their problems. Robert Ferralasco mentioned one particular individual whose drinking earned him a nickname:

66 He must have been one of the first ones drafted and spent his entire five or six years being shot at and hit a number of times. He was shell-shocked. We called him 'Whiskey' Jones. He really earned that honor because he stayed drunk just every day. Somehow he got to most of his classes, but I don't know that he ever passed anything. He consumed so much bourbon. 99

Tex Plunkett recalled an incident in which a veteran was reformed of alcohol consumption, at least for the duration of his time on campus:

66 One morning one of my students that lived in a house on what we called Billy Goat Hill . . . called me and said, 'Tex, you've got to do something. There is some women up here, and one of them called the police, and old [student's name deleted] is down there just naked as a jaybird playing Tarzan in the trees.' Now those trees is down by the railroad tracks about where the fire station is. I jumped in the car and went down, and sure enough, he was naked as a jaybird, just swinging around having the best time you have ever saw. We grabbed him and got his

underwear on him and slapped him two or three times, told him he was in big trouble. He kind of sobered up. He had been there all night long, and so I got him in the backseat and told him to lie down. 99

As bad luck would have it, more excitement was in store. Plunkett continued:

66 I started up Caraway Road with him, and just as we crossed the railroad tracks nearest to the university, we met the police with the dean of men going to look for him. I waved at them and kept driving, and we got up to what is now a rose garden, then an old building. Upstairs was empty and had some old mattresses, and I unloaded him there and told him to stay there because he was in big trouble. He was sober enough to understand. I don't know how long he stayed there. That was on Sunday, and I didn't see him again until Tuesday when he came into my office and said, 'Tex, I guess I really made a fool of myself.' He was a World War II veteran, and a great many of those veterans had been taught to drink, especially if they had been flyers. They were met with plenty of whiskey, which is supposed to relax them after the experience, and he had been one of them. He apologized all over the place, and I said for him to think nothing of it. Just be careful and don't do it again. As far as I know, he never took another drink while he was on the campus. 99

Many veterans were family men with children. Consequently, they could not be housed in the residence halls. The solution to this difficulty was the construction of a trailer village on Caraway Street across from Danner Hall. Ike Tomlinson described the deplorable condition of these trailers:

66 The things were flimsy. . . . Inadequate laundry facilities. Some of the faculty's wives just raised sin about how those girls had to live over there. But I didn't know anything else could have been done. We had to make do with what we could at that time. 99

Bill Davidson, who with his wife resided in this temporary housing in the early fifties, had

vivid memories of the cramped conditions of the trailers:

66 The trailers that we lived in might have been eight by fifteen or sixteen [feet]. . . . When you walked into the door of the trailer, there was a couch that folded out and that was your bed. In the middle of it you had an apartment-sized little gas range, a sink, and behind you . . . was an ice box. You put a sign up in your window every day that you wanted a . . . block of ice. He [the iceman] didn't have to knock or anything. He just came in. In the back one-third [of the trailer] there was just a little table and chair, and that was all. There was a little closet back there. 99

Although Davidson and his fellow residents of trailer city paid only fifteen dollars per month rent, this amount appeared formidable in that day.

Despite the difficulties they posed, the veterans solved the enrollment problems for Arkansas State College. But the instability that characterized most of the 1940s for ASC went beyond enrollment problems. Shake-ups at the administrative level left faculty and supporters of the institution with a sense of unease.

In January 1943, V.C. Kays resigned as chief executive of the institution after 34 years. He was succeeded by Horace Thompson, who had graduated from Aggie in 1925 and then from the University of Arkansas. Thompson's abrupt resignation in June 1945 left the college virtually leaderless. President Emeritus Kays, who had been serving as business manager, returned to service temporarily, but he could not make long range plans for the college.

The board of trustees hoped that a new president would restore confidence in the college and continue the progress that Kays had initiated during his first term in office. Their choice for the new president was William J. Edens, a man of impeccable credentials who assumed office in 1946. Edens graduated from Mississippi State College and received a doctorate in agricultural economics from Cornell University. He taught at Cornell and Western Kentucky University before returning to Mississippi State as assistant to the dean of agriculture.

Many of Edens' contemporaries had positive recollections of the school's third president. Mildred Vance, professor of elementary education, viewed him as a "very pleasant, a real calm type person." William V. Wyatt, who became a member of the board of trustees at Arkansas State while Edens was president, characterized him as "a dedicated educator." John Galloway, professor of history, perceived Edens as a "gentleman of the old school . . . an old southern gentleman." Wanda Walker,

associate professor of English, thought he was "always very serious minded" and that "he was rather fair."

In spite of these positive attributes, Edens did not have a particularly successful five years at Arkansas State. Certainly the school made some significant progress during those years, particularly in student affairs, the development of an extension program, and the growth of the athletic program. But Edens lacked Kays' political

The student body during the war years consisted primarily of women. Pictured here is an art class conducted by Mrs. Daniel F. Pasmore (fourth from left) in the early 1940s.

savvy and the ability to deal with people in anything but a formal manner. Lou Couch spoke of the latter feature of Edens' character:

66 It just seemed like that he didn't know how to handle people like a man in that position should. He was not too stand-offish, but still he somehow had a vision or an image of what a college president—what he thought it should be. This kind of kept him a little bit aloof. 99

John Galloway concluded that some of Edens' problems arose from his excessive formality:

66 I think Dr. Edens' formality and strict attention to administrative affairs on the campus hurt him with the community. He also was engaged in a very bitter battle over appropriations from the legislature. This was a time when we had pulled pretty well ahead of the other four-year state colleges and were still getting the same appropriations annually from the legislature. And Dr. Edens felt this was very unfair and set out to correct this wrong and encountered some very stiff opposition. It took him several years to persuade the legislature to establish a . . . bit larger appropriations. 99

At the same time, Galloway thought of President Edens as a man devoted to scholarship and to making the resources of the college available to the people of northeast Arkansas. The history professor participated with Edens in a lecture series sponsored by the Singer Company in Trumann, twenty miles southeast of Jonesboro, and recalled that Edens frequently participated in such programs and encouraged the faculty to do so.

Many students recalled the president's excessive desire for neatness and tidiness of campus grounds. Robert Ferralasco observed Edens' concern with appearance:

66 Dr. Edens in those days was quite concerned about such important things as keeping off the grass. He spent a good bit of his time talking about how we were mistreating the buildings and the fact that we were not walking on the sidewalks. . . . He was always doing things to

keep us off the grass. I remember one morning we got up real early to a horrible odor in the air. What he had done was he had brought in very fresh fertilizer from—manure, I suppose you'd call it. I'm not quite sure what it was, but it was horrible. He spread it all over the campus, and it was rather difficult with no air conditioning in those days to sit in class—even your dormitory room—with windows open. We needed the windows open for the air. I think he chuckled over that for a long time. 99

The matter of campus cleanliness was a recurrent theme in Edens' talks with students. Eugene Smith, a student at ASC in the late 1940s, spoke of the usual content of the president's messages:

66 He used to admonish us for deposited paper and litter around campus. . . . I guess the one thing I remember was his concern for the appearance of the campus. 99

Eleanor Lane, a faculty member at the time, remembered that he did more than talk about campus beautification: "They put a large flower bed on the west side of Wilson. And, of course, the students immediately called it the 'Garden of Edens.' "

The events that led to Edens' resignation were complex. Among the contributing factors were his own personal traits, the political enemies he had made in his efforts to secure more funding for the institution, antagonism from some members of the college faculty, and general factionalism among his supporters and detractors.

Although Edens' supporters and opponents struggled for a majority on the board of trustees, he realized that his effectiveness on the ASC campus was coming to an end. Robert Moore, a new administrative staff member during the turmoil, reported:

66 Dr. Edens took a job in Saudi Arabia with a Point Four agricultural appointment in one of these government programs overseas. . . . Dr. Edens never came back to this campus. 99

Two members of the faculty recalled the meeting in 1951 at which President Edens

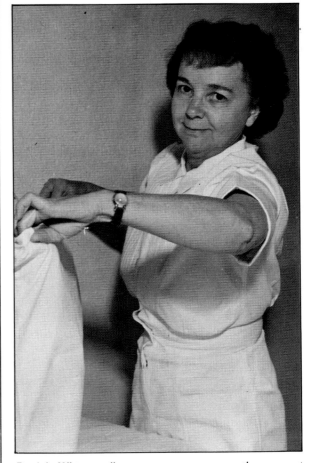

Beulah White, college nurse, was among the support personnel who assisted students at ASC during the 1940s.

Despite the war effort, which drained the campus of male students, work on the ASC farms continued. In addition to milking being a chore, female students at ASC participated in milking contests.

Ruth Bryan Owen (center in lower right photo), daughter of William Jennings Bryan, visited campus in 1949 for an international relations seminar. Mrs. Owen was the alternate U.S. representative to the United Nations and was the first woman to hold a diplomatic post in the U.S. Foreign Service.

announced his resignation. The response was equally factionalized. Wanda Walker remembered, "One person who was on the faculty at the time just jumped to her feet and started clapping and hoorahing. It was quite a spectacle, I assure you." Mildred Vance recalled a much different kind of reaction among some faculty members: "And at that time many of the faculty members started crying. . . . I really believe that the faculty felt that he was a very good friend." The departure of William J. Edens and the appointment of Carl R. Reng as his successor ended a decade of instability.

Yet clearly the final verdict on Edens' role as college executive has not been delivered. In spite of his problems, Edens was bringing the college back to a time of progress and development. Advancement occurred in both academic and extra-curricular activities. For the presence of veterans or of administrative turmoil did not prevent the institution from continuing and reviving the activities it had begun before the war.

The demonstration school, established in the 1920s to train public school teachers, continued to flourish. Lebelva Connelly, a training school teacher, had fond memories of her work in the late 1940s. She recalled a senior trip to Memphis:

66 The high school seniors . . . would get what they called a 'skip day.' . . . When they talked to me about taking them, I said, 'Well, I'll help you organize a day, but it must be a "skip day." I'm not taking one or two. If you all want to go, we'll organize one, and I'll ask to chaperone you. We'll go one day. But it must be something you remember with the senior class you'll be graduating with in high school.' 99

Students and sponsor made the trip to Memphis in a school bus driven by Ralph Waddell. "And we took off for Memphis," Connelly continued:

66 Went down to Front Street, and there was the *Prairie Schooner*. And they were all looking for us, and I loaded my kids on. They were just fascinated. Many of them had never seen the Mississippi [River]. 99

The college solved the problem of housing for returning servicemen and their families by placing small house trailers and a communal laundry north of the present location of the Carl R. Reng Center.

The group from the training school then visited such sites in the Tennessee city as the Brooks Art Gallery, the Overton Park Zoo, and the Pink Palace Museum. They all had a fine dinner at a restaurant in downtown Memphis. This memorable experience was immortalized on film as Connelly noted:

66 There's still pictures around of a giraffe or camel or something with its head stuck up, and I'm standing there outside the fence. And they say, 'The little one is our English teacher.' 99

One of the most notable innovations of the Edens' administration in the late 1940s was the creation of an extension program. This program aimed to serve rural communities that had little access to any institution of higher learning. That was the task for which Robert Moore was hired in 1949. Moore summarized how the program was started:

66 I started the extension division that printed the first extension catalog. We set up the first correspondence courses during that year. Got faculty members to write courses. We put out a catalog, mailed it out to people. I stayed on the road a whole lot at night organizing extension courses and then came back and tried to con some faculty member to go out and teach it at a nominal fee, not much. But there was a little money, and all of them wanted to do it. 99

One person who benefited from the new program was Gladys Hudgins, who later joined the faculty of ASC's physical education department. She taught in Swifton, Arkansas, at the time and attended ASC extension classes that were offered in nearby Newport. She recalled:

66 It might be a course in English. . . . It might be a course in history or social science or whatever. It was always teachers at that time earning extension hours because a lot of teachers did not have degrees at that time. 99

She praised the courses, but noted that attending them had its drawbacks:

" The extension courses were well put together, but it was very difficult for a full-time teacher to make the preparation they needed to. So that was a disadvantage to me. That plus lack of involvement on campus—access to a library and that sort of thing. "

The other side of the extension courses, the labors of the instructors themselves, was presented by W.L. Smith:

" We would go out to organize a class, and some of them would meet once a week. Sometimes they would meet twice a week. You might teach one course, or you might teach two at a time. You might teach one class, have a break, and then go teach a different one. We did it both ways. But some of us took some pretty long trips—I remember I taught at Hayti, Missouri, and I believe it was eighty miles. So you drove a hundred and sixty miles round trip. Get back well after midnight. "

At the same time Smith was teaching eighteen semester hours on the Jonesboro campus.

Paul Couch, head of the education department and later first director of the institution's graduate program, recalled the benefits that extension work brought to the university. As he said:

" It's surprising how many of those people [extension students] eventually came down and got their degrees. One class up in Senath [Missouri] I know because they came and told me that. 'Now all of us got through [at ASC] except one.' . . . We had to have them to keep the college open. There was no question about that. . . . Not only that, but those people had kids, and they sent those kids down here eventually. "

Coach J.A. "Ike" Tomlinson (right in top photo), resurrected the intercollegiate athletic program in 1945, handling the job of athletic director and football, baseball, and basketball coach. The following year, Forrest "Frosty" England (lower photo) was hired to take over the football coaching duties.

Members of the local Delta Omega Sigma fraternity and their dates enjoy dinner at the Peabody Hotel in Memphis during the summer of 1946.

The time that faculty members devoted to their classes seems staggering by today's standards. As W.L. Smith recalled, "First summer I taught here . . . I had a course that ended at four o'clock. On Saturday afternoon." A typical teaching load for a faculty member during the fall or spring semester might be as many as eighteen hours (six courses) in addition to extension classes taught at night in some community in northeast Arkansas or southeast Missouri. Yet the faculty that ASC was able to attract in these post-war years, in Paul Couch's words, "formed a nucleus . . . of fine teachers in all departments to make us a good liberal arts college." These able faculty members came to the college despite the heavy teaching responsibilities and relatively low salaries, and many of them stayed on the staff for many years.

One of the most memorable of these dedicated faculty members was Dean B. Ellis, a Vanderbilt University graduate who taught mathematics to several generations of Aggie and ASC students. Member of a wealthy Jonesboro family, Ellis had joined the faculty at First District Agricultural and Mechanical College in 1926. Both students and colleagues praised his ability. He was "a genius at mathematics," according to Mildred Vance; "as broad a man as I have ever known" and "a brilliant mathematician," in the estimation of Marshall Matthews; and "a perfectionist," said Buddy Kays.

The circumstances that compelled Ellis to teach at Aggie were related to Buddy Kays by his father:

❝ The legislature had passed a bill [in 1926] that you couldn't teach anything about [Charles] Darwin's theories in [public] schools—couldn't teach evolution. So uptown at the high school, they had an old janitor spying on them kind of listening at the door, and he reported Dean for teaching evolution. They called Dean in, and Dean [replied that he] was talking about the evolution of mathematics. So with that short temper of his, he came on out here. Daddy said he walked in the office, sat down, and said, 'You got a job?' Daddy said, 'We got one, but we can't pay you what you are getting up there.' He said, 'I don't care.' ❞

Ellis practiced a simple, yet direct teaching method, one that his students later pursued in their educational careers. Marshall Matthews concluded that math instructors would do well to return to Ellis' methods:

❝ Dean Ellis would tell you that to teach an average freshman, he needs to be given an

A tradition that continued for many years, the "daisy chain," was observed as part of graduation ceremonies in the 1940s and 1950s. The chain symbolized the bonds between students and was passed from the shoulders of the seniors to the shoulders of the juniors to symbolize transfer of campus responsibilities.

assignment, some coaching and then sent to the blackboard, and you watch him perform and help him correct his mistakes as he goes along, and I firmly believe that. Mathematics you can't talk it into them. ❞

Eugene Smith, an English major, was happy with a B from Ellis' trigonometry class:

❝ He was demanding. He expected you to have done your homework. Being an English major, college algebra and trigonometry was the extent of my mathematics that I took at the collegiate level. . . . He believed very much in blackboard work. If he sent you to the board to work the problems of the day and you were not prepared to do so, he would pitch a fit. Sometimes he would throw an eraser at you. He also could be very understanding if you did not understand. ❞

DAY OF THE BIG "SMOKE DOMPAH DAY"

SIGMA PI

The late 1940s saw the formation of national fraternity and sorority chapters on the ASC campus. Alpha Pi Chapter of Sigma Pi was chartered in 1948, followed the next week by Delta Theta Chapter of Pi Kappa Alpha. Epsilon Zeta Chapter of Alpha Gamma Delta sorority also appeared in 1948.

His outbursts of profanity, punctuated by the hurling of chalk or an eraser, became a subject of much discussion. Tex Plunkett related the experience of one inattentive student:

❝ One day he was at the board demonstrating an equation, and an old boy—he came from up in the hills. I think he just came down to play football. He was in that class and evidently had been out quite late the night before. He would nod and once went to sleep, and Dean Ellis turned around and picked up an eraser—back in those days the backs were made out of wood—and hit the kid up the side of the head. He didn't go to sleep anymore after that. . . . When he was really concentrating, he didn't like to be disturbed. One day a boy knocked his books off in class and made quite a clatter. He picked them up, and I don't know how it happened, but he knocked them off again. Dean Ellis came over and said, 'I'll help you,' and picked up all the boy's books and pitched them out the window and told him that 'they won't bother you anymore.' ❞

This salty professor often employed crude and blunt imagery to make a point for a student. If Ellis' purpose was to humble the young scholars, he certainly succeeded. Phil Bridger remembered that a good friend emerged deflated one day:

❝ I can remember my best buddy was going to make a doctor or something, and to be honest with you I think they spotted it right off he didn't have the talent. He was in Dean Ellis' class and had him do something, and I never will forget Dean Ellis telling him, 'Well, I've got a dog at home that I can train quicker than I can you.' He dropped out of pre-med and made a career in [military] service and has done real well. Dean

Ellis was one that had the reputation that if you can get it, you get it. If you can't, you better drop it in a hurry. **"**

To Elmer Mayes, who declared that Ellis' demands for blackboard work gave him fallen arches, the crusty mathematician employed equally brutalizing words. Both Ellis and Mayes were pilots. After one very unsuccessful attempt at blackboard work, the exasperated instructor turned to the pupil and declared:

" Elmer, one of these days you're going to be coming in for a landing. They're going to signal you to not land, and you're going to come in and kill yourself. **"**

Just as often this domineering professor would follow such withering outbursts with a stroke of brilliance that would astound the class. Buddy Kays related an instance when Dean B. Ellis (students often mistook his name "Dean" for the academic title) used the presence of a foreign student to make a point:

" We had a Chinese student in those days. . . . Of course, foreign students were kind of a rarity in those days, and there was no integration as far as blacks were concerned. This fellow [was] from China, Yee Tin Boo. He's still in this country down in Huntsville, Albama. But . . . one of the things that Dean did was to call him up to the board and ask him to put a Chinese character up there—anything. The point he was trying to make was on symbols. You could use X, Y, or anything you assigned a value to it. He used that right along with his teaching math. **"**

Clarissa Delano, who was employed as an instructor in government and sociology in 1946, also exercised quite an impact upon the student body. Robert Ferralasco recounted an anecdote which illustrates both the instructor's dedication to classroom learning and perhaps a bit of her frontier upbringing on the cold Nebraska prairie:

" It was November. They said that the boiler or something had broken down. Dr. Edens had suggested to the teachers that if the students complained for them to check the roll and spend

a few minutes going over assignments and then letting them go so they might go back to their dormitory where it was a little bit warmer. Miss Delano, bless her heart, just didn't believe in those kind of things. **"**

One day Ferralasco and his classmates were struggling to listen to Miss Delano's lecture and keep warm at the same time, when several girls urged him to protest this uncomfortable situation:

" I raised my hand and said, 'Miss Delano . . . I think the girls are awfully cold in class, and they'd like permission to leave.' She kind of looked a little upset about that and said if I didn't like the way she was running her class, I should go see Dr. Edens. Well, that's the wrong thing to tell a veteran, you know. I got up and said, 'Thank you, ma'am. I believe I will.' **"**

However, the beleaguered teacher shrewdly decided to send a committee to visit the president, not just the firebrand Ferralasco. When the three-person committee presented their case to Dr. Edens, he laughed, much to their surprise. "The man didn't laugh very often," said

Ferralasco. Edens gave the committee a note for Miss Delano to read to the class. "So we took the note up, and Miss Delano read the note to the class saying that if anyone was cold, they might leave," Ferralasco concluded. "And, of course, we all got up and walked out." He then related another incident which involved Miss Delano's classroom relations with students:

" One time one of the students brought his pet snake to class, and Miss Delano does not like snakes, we found out. He let it go on the floor, and the snake went crawling around, and she went running out the door screaming, and the girls in the class screamed. I thought that was so adolescent. I got particularly upset with the fellow when I felt something crawling around, and I reached my hand in and he had put it inside my shirt—the snake. I followed Miss Delano out the door. **"**

Clearly the level of humor in student pranks on teachers had not changed much at Arkansas State since William Troy Martin had frightened Zenobia Brumbaugh with a snake some thirty years previously.

The Marching Indian Band was created in the late 1940s under the direction of James L. Patty.

Pearl J. Essary served the campus for many years as postmistress. The post office was located during the 1940s in the basement of Wilson Hall.

Perhaps the most memorable feature of Miss Delano's career at ASC was her ineptitude behind the wheel of an automobile. Ferralasco neatly summed up the effects of Miss Delano at the wheel of her big green car: "Some of the most exciting things that have happened on the college campus occurred while she was learning to drive and after she learned to drive." Her automobile became recognizable not only to college students, but to townspeople as well:

❝ I think that's probably the only thing that saved her life and a lot of other lives because as she drove in town, people saw the green car coming, and everyone got out of her way. She just absolutely could not control that car. ❞

While the college was preparing for the expansion that would soon occur, student life was returning to the normal prewar routine. The practice of hazing freshmen assumed new dimensions. Eugene Smith noted, "Freshmen had to attire themselves in certain ways, including a beanie on their head, until after the homecoming game." Furthermore, all freshmen "were supposed to parade through downtown Jonesboro in their pajamas and their beanies." Smith claimed that he and his friends balked at this exercise and regarded it as "beneath the dignity of college folks."

A major development in student life in the late 1940s was the organization of social fraternities and sororities that were affiliated with national organizations. Robert Moore recalled how that came about:

❝ Just as I came here, we were beginning the Greek organizations. There had been local organizations here that formed back in the late thirties, sort of wildcat. Mr. Kays evidently didn't believe in many organizations. But they formed some local groups, and in 1948 two groups became national. PiKA and Sigma Pi came on the campus and took over two of the old fraternities. . . . Two of the sororities combined and made what is now Alpha Gam, and one of them made what is now AOPi. And TKE came in the next year. ❞

The Herald, *which was edited and printed on campus, continued to spread the news about ASC.*

Robert Ferralasco vividly recollected fraternity hazing during the period:

❝ They didn't hesitate using the paddle and the belt. It was amazing that we would stand for it, those of us who had been in the service, but we did. We took our licks, and we did some crazy things. For instance, the worst thing that our fraternity did, besides making us dress like girls and shining shoes during the week of hell week—they would give us a list of half-a-dozen people, and we were taken blindfolded, driven all over the country, most of us from out of town, not from Jonesboro, not knowing where we were. We were released in a graveyard. We were not to come back until we got the names off the tombstones. Many times they would give you several fictitious ones just to make sure you stayed out all night. ❞

In 1942, it was still "no cars allowed" for most students. Students such as Joyce Lichtenberger McEwen found a bicycle to be a convenient way of getting around the growing campus.

An important change in student affairs occurred when Edens authorized a student government. Robert Moore described the situation when he arrived on campus in 1949: "They had no elected student government." Instead the presidents of fifteen student organizations comprised a student council. They, in turn, elected their chairman, who became president of the student council. But, as Moore explained, this rudimentary organization "didn't lend itself to any participation and no respect for the students of any kind." He worked out a solution:

❝ I went to the president, and he agreed to let us write a constitution. Dr. John Galloway . . . and Dr. [Chester] Carrothers [head of the business administration department] and a couple of students and myself—we worked on it and wrote a constitution. ❞

The appearance of the Student Government Association represented a clear realization that the student body had rights and a place on campus.

There were still rules and regulations the students adhered to and the faculty and staff enforced. However, perhaps because of the veterans' influence, these statutes were not as stringently enforced as they had been. Eleanor Lane, associate professor of English, cited some instances of faculty regulation of student behavior. She recalled:

❝ [Faculty members] would drop in at night on some of these boys that had an apartment uptown. And if they had wild parties or something like that, why, they would be called on the carpet immediately for their behavior if they were not living in a manner that the administrators thought they should be living. ❞

The athletic program at ASC had all but died during World War II. All able-bodied men, of course, participated in the war. Few players were available. The college did not field teams in football or other sports in 1942, 1943, and 1944. Ike Tomlinson reactivated the teams after the war and coached several sports. He described the conditions that led to the restoration of ASC football:

❝ In late '44 I was called in and asked if I would accept the director of physical education and athletics job—that they were going to reinstitute some athletics which had been dropped during the war. They were going to expand the physical education program and try to get more people, and the civilian draft was beginning to slow down a little bit. So I accepted that job and went from there to restoration of football in '45. . . . We had a total of twenty-one men actually that reported. Seventeen stayed out, and our first game was with Ouachita Baptist. We had thirteen able to play. ❞

Perhaps northeast Arkansas was not ready for the return of college athletics so soon after the war, for Tomlinson recalled that few people attended these early games: "I don't believe that we ever had a gate that exceeded $200." His football budget for that first year was only $1,100.

Post-war athletics at ASC, particularly football, came into its own when Tomlinson hired Forrest W. "Frosty" England as head football coach. An expert on the T-formation, England came to Arkansas State in 1946 and remained until 1953. During that time he never had a losing season and took the ASC Indians to four post-season bowl games. England is probably the most well-remembered of any coach at the institution. Tex Plunkett had a clear impression of England's coaching abilities:

❝ Frosty England, I believe, could get more out of a team and the team like him less until after they had won a game than any coach I've ever known. . . . He modeled himself, I think, after what he had read about Knute Rockne, and he did everything before a game—everything in his power to demean a boy. He would line them up and tell them they were going to run all over them. And by the time the game started, his team was like a bunch of quivering racehorses. They just couldn't wait to get in there and kill somebody. He really had a tender side to him, too. ❞

Gladys Hudgins characterized England as a "gentleman first-class" and cited his excellent performance in the classroom. Unlike members of coaching staffs today, England taught twelve hours virtually every semester. Hudgins, who sponsored cheerleaders for several of England's teams in the early fifties, recalled that the coach became "an entirely different person when he was on the football field." She attended one of the bowl games that England coached: "I don't believe part of the time he knew what was going on. He got so beside himself. His assistants were running the game at that stage of it." Phil Bridger, who was a training school student at the time, looked up to Coach England "in awe."

When England began the 1946 season at ASC, he faced a major problem: lack of equipment. He recollected, "Their equipment was nil—practically been disposed of during those war years when the Army was in here and based here on the campus." Orders for equipment had been sent to firms in St. Louis, but there was little hope that the orders could be filled in time for the first game. England related the fortuitous circumstances that allowed him to equip his team in the nick of time for their first outing:

" At that time I was sort of a pioneer in the split T-formation and lectured at clinics all over this country. And I had a T-formation clinic coming up in . . . Fremont, Michigan. . . . This was to last all day. So we started the morning session. I remember telling them I was just happy to be there and would tell them everything I knew and thought about the T-formation. And asked if they would please do one favor for me in return. 'What's that?' 'Tell me where I can buy some football equipment.' **"**

During an intermission one of England's listeners referred him to Dad Harder "at the House of Harder in Goshen, Indiana." England found that Harder indeed had the equipment. He continued his story:

" We drove from Fremont, Michigan, to Goshen, Indiana, and I met the most gracious, understanding, compassionate man called Dad Harder and his family. They had a rather large

A version of "Jumping Joe" had already become a campus symbol and mascot by the late 1940s.

Bus trips to Memphis and St. Louis afforded students and faculty opportunities to attend the opera and other cultural events.

business in athletic supplies. And when I entered the store, I thought, 'Well, I've been disappointed again because this place doesn't have any amount of athletic supplies for a team.' But he took me down to the basement, and the walls were lined and the shelves filled down throughout the basement. And he said, 'How much equipment will you need?' 'Well,' I said, 'We need about sixty complete outfits.' 🙮

So Dad Harder supplied the equipment for England's first game as head coach at Arkansas State College.

Many of England's football players were war veterans, and coaching them presented challenges that differed from the problems coaches normally faced. England claimed:

🙮 Coaching has always been a laboratory for dealing with all kinds of sociological, psychological problems. And with the veterans, they brought their share. 🙮

He settled family squabbles among married veterans, kept the peace in the trailer village, and dealt with a group of men who had had all the discipline they were willing to endure in military service. Ike Tomlinson told of one veteran who presented some special problems for the coaching staff:

🙮 It was a very heinous thing for an athlete to have a drink back then of alcoholic beverage. I had one football player to walk in and tell me that 'Now, coach, I've been living on whiskey for four years. Now, I'm not about to give it up now.' He was just that frank. You thought about that, and it seemed terrible until he began telling you why he had whiskey and some of the places he had been. 🙮

Yet coaching veterans was not entirely a negative experience. England testified that "the men that I had . . . were pretty fine people." One of the veterans stood out in England's memory:

🙮 Harry Larche was a veteran. He'd never played football in high school. He practiced three

Dr. D.F. Pasmore's French and German classes observed the Yule log tradition each Christmas with a party in the Commons Building. The Yule log cake, iced with chocolate and complete with knots, was the centerpiece for the party. Spanish students were treated to a Mexican pinata party.

days there in the heat. One day he said, 'Coach, I'm going to have to quit.' I said, 'You're not going to quit, but what is the problem?' 'Well,' he said, 'I just can't stand this equipment.' And he held his chin up. His chin was just raw. He had his shoulder pads on backwards. Had been practicing in that heat for three days. And I said, 'You go in there and get some powder and ointment under your chin and wrapped up a bit and put your shoulder pads on this way, Harry.' And he did. Harry graduated from college in three years, taking eighteen hours a semester. Was married. Had a child. And when he finished playing for me, he was signed to a professional football contract. Played in the Blue-Gray game down in Montgomery, Alabama. Later I hired him as assistant coach. He was with me for several years. When I left Arkansas State, he went with me to the University of Toledo. 🙮

Out-of-town trips by the football teams added an element of excitement during the late 1940s. Robert Ferralasco, who was team manager, recalled one such trip to Cincinnati:

🙮 We were, I'd say, a hundred or something miles outside of Cincinnati, and the bus broke down. Well, we hadn't eaten lunch. The [coaches'] cars were so far ahead. We had no idea where they were. No one had any money except a little pocket change. We'd stop out in the countryside, of course. Naturally, we didn't have any choice as to where the bus was going to break down. I remember going into some fields there. There must have been some kind of fruit still on the trees. . . . We waited around for awhile. Several had hitchhiked up to the next town and back to the past town trying to get to a phone to call ahead. We knew the name of the hotel in

The Faculty Women's Club Christmas Dinner, held in the Commons Building, was an opportunity for the entire faculty to get together to socialize. Faculty children were included and often provided the entertainment since many of them attended the training school.

Cincinnati where we were supposed to be. In fact, we should have been there by then. No answer from anyone. No help or aid, so we decided we would let everyone fare for himself. Well, you can imagine having a full football team out on the road strung out a hundred miles between a broken-down bus and the hotel in Cincinnati. **"**

Ferralasco arrived at the hotel about eleven o'clock that night to find the coach fuming. "I think around one o'clock was about the latest that some of the football players arrived." He added:

" I think it did affect our play because the next day at half-time it was zero to zero, and we obviously had better personnel. But finally we lost the game, maybe two to nothing or seven, but very, very low-scoring game. I think the fellows just gave out. **"**

The growing interest in the athletic program spawned complementary activities. James L. Patty organized a band of about twenty-five musicians who had only sweaters for uniforms. Ferralasco described homecoming floats built by students who would "stay up all night" and miss classes only to have their creation "topple over."

Thus the decade of the 1940s had been traumatic for ASC. The upheavals caused by drastic enrollment fluctuations, the need to adapt to new kinds of students, and the changes in the administration left their mark. But the essential health of the institution was evident in that campus life began to reestablish itself in the familiar routines. By the time Carl R. Reng became president in 1951, most of the real instability attributable to the dislocation of war and the post-war readjustment had ended. The institution was now ready to pursue the goal of expansion.

A common sight on campus was botany professor Delzie Demaree collecting plant specimens.

The two longest tenured presidents in Arkansas State's history, Carl Reng (left) and V.C. Kays (right), talk with Judge W.M. Thompson of Batesville. Thompson was one of the legislative leaders in founding A-State in 1909.

President Reng enjoyed the support of the board of trustees for many years. Shown at a 1952 board meeting are (from left) Roland Hughes, James Heath, college attorney Berl Smith, Russell Owen, William Wyatt, R.S. Rainwater, and Reng.

The 1950s and early 1960s were remarkable for the growth of Arkansas State College. This burgeoning of the campus was all the more remarkable, considering the stagnation of the previous decade. Many reasons account for the abrupt turnabout. In 1951, Carl R. Reng assumed the presidency and introduced an energetic administration. A more enlightened attitude among state and federal officials contributed greatly to the growth of Arkansas State and other educational institutions. New attitudes among leaders stemmed partly from a sincere realization that a college degree produced a more useful citizen, but also from a fear of the spread of communism—the first major challenge to Western democracy on a global scale. State and federal appropriations for higher education flowed much more freely. In popular thinking in eastern Arkansas, the college degree replaced the high school diploma as a prerequisite for long-term career plans. After World War II, the average person was educated to expect more material prosperity from life, and the four-year degree was essential to that goal. The growth of rapid transportation continued to tie the hinterland more closely to Arkansas State College. To commute fifty or sixty miles each day (not just on weekends) became common.

The boom these many forces provoked at Arkansas State was reflected in numerous ways. Not only did the enrollment climb dramatically, but the physical plant that V.C. Kays so laboriously constructed in the 1930s became inadequate. College officials purchased new acreage. The faculty grew in size and sophistication, while the number of employees in the administration and service areas grew proportionately. The curriculum broadened to include graduate degree programs. What was once a "cow college" with a heavy emphasis on agricultural education gave way to a many-sided course catalog.

This era of growth was closely associated with the presidency of Carl Raymond Reng. An Iowan by birth, he received a bachelor of arts degree from Buena Vista College in 1932, taught public school, and served in the Navy in World War II. He departed the Navy with the rank of lieutenant commander and earned a doctor of education degree from the University of Missouri in 1948. While teaching in the education department at the University of Arkansas, Reng's name came to the attention of the board of trustees of Arkansas State College. The school was searching for a replacement for William J. Edens, who had recently resigned. William Wyatt, a former student and faculty member, was then serving on the board. He recalled the circumstances that led to an interview with Reng:

❝ We thought we did a real good job in getting Dr. Reng. . . . Fred Pickens had some word of him, and Orville Cheney's son had been at the university that year, and he knew him . . . [from] his work up there in the graduate school, I believe. That's where we contacted him, and he came down. I remember one thing he told us when he came down here. He said, 'If you ask me to do this, I'm going to do it. I'm not going to be an errand boy.' That suited us because that's what we wanted, somebody to take charge and do it. ❞

The prospective president's recollection of this meeting was substantially the same:

❝ So one evening the president of the board—Orville Cheney . . . called me and asked me if I'd be interested in the presidency over here. And I said, 'Well, sure, I'm always interested.' I didn't know if I'd be or not. I'd had a great number of students from this area in my graduate program at the University of Arkansas. I

A landmark in A-State's growth of prestige was the selection of the Marching Indians and the Drill Team to represent the State of Arkansas at the inauguration of President John F. Kennedy in 1961.

In the early 1950s, the secondary level training school was closed and laboratory schools were set up in five surrounding communities. This first meeting of the Secondary Student Teacher Training Program was held in the fall of 1952 in the Commons Building to organize the outlying laboratory programs.

was in charge of a graduate program there in education, and they had been the ones that had told Cheney that I might be interested. So I came over here, and I flew over on a Sunday and got here about ten o'clock in the morning, and by two o'clock that afternoon they had offered me the position and I had taken it. **"**

The new president's wife was surprised and somewhat dismayed at the news:

" My wife wasn't too happy about it. We had just bought a new home in Fayetteville. She said, 'Oh, my goodness, we just got this home settled and now moving.' I said, 'Well, one thing for sure.' I said, 'I think I can last one year over there, and when we retire and sit on the front porch of the poor house, you can always say I was president.' **"**

When Reng arrived to take up his post in 1951, he immediately set about the selection of persons for his administration. These officials remained with him for many years and formed a close-knit group upon whom he could depend for loyalty. Ray Hall, one of Reng's former students at the University of Arkansas, became director of field services. Linual Cameron became director of finance. Hall recalled the institution when he arrived on August 31, 1951:

" On hand at this school at that time was really a community of scholars. They were more or less like one big family. The school consisted of seventeen divisions. There were no colleges and department heads as such. As I recall, there were about 712 students. In the catalog, they only listed sixty-one persons on the faculty and staff. **"**

The new president and his staff soon concluded that several fundamental flaws existed in the method of state funding of higher education. These handicaps must be remedied before Arkansas State College could grow. The state assembly allocated equal revenues to this institution and its three counterparts at Monticello, Russellville, and Magnolia under the provisions of the 1909 law. This statute—by now far out-of-date—seriously restricted the college's ability to accommodate the growing enrollment of the

Elementary school-age children disappeared from the campus in the early fifties with the elimination of the ASC Training School. This 1951 class was directed by Mildred Vance (far left) and Lillian Barton (far right).

1950s. The pace of this growth also far exceeded the rate of increase at the sister colleges. Reng gave Cameron the go-ahead to find a means to persuade the state legislature to abandon this restrictive part of Act 100. The common term used to describe this method of appropriation was "lock-step." Cameron's first move consisted of an effort to convince state education officials in Little Rock that Arkansas State's enrollment figures were genuine and accurate. State officials were skeptical about these statistics because colleges often inflated enrollment numbers to obtain more funds. "Now I'll tell you this . . . ," declared Cameron. "We never lied about enrollment; never lied to the legislature."

Once this first obstacle had been overcome, ASC's authorities began a campaign to persuade the legislature to accept a new method of funding higher education in Arkansas—a formula system. This formula would award funds, in part based upon the number of students enrolled, multiplied by the number of hours (generally each course met three hours weekly) each student registered for during a semester. Cameron believed that some support for a formula existed in Little Rock, since such a reasonable means of allocating funds would be attractive to taxpayers, but the campaign for more equitable treatment was not easy. Cameron recalled:

❝ We went to the legislature, and I said 'Dr. Reng, do you want to try it?' He said, 'Yes.' I said, 'Well, now let me explain what will happen.' I said, 'We won't have a friend in the legislature among the other colleges or what have you.' I said, 'It is going to get rough. It is going to get down to the dealy-wheely personality. It's going to be the roughest thing you have ever been into.' I said, 'Now, when we get in it, there is no looking back. . . . Knowing what I'm telling you, do you still want to go into it?' And he said, 'Yes.' ❞

This struggle continued for many years, and the new administration soon concluded that the state legislature failed to comprehend Arkansas State College's situation within the scheme of higher education in the state. The distant location of ASC in a remote corner of Arkansas contributed to difficulties in convincing the powers-that-be in the state capitol that A-State was no longer a small agricultural high school confined to the First District, as the 1909 law envisioned the campus. Cameron said:

❝ Northeast Arkansas to a large extent belonged to Memphis, and Memphis was where the people in northeast Arkansas traded. They never went to Little Rock, and what we had to do [was] convince the rest of the state that we were not—the school did not belong to Jonesboro—that it belonged to the whole state. It was a state institution. That was a hard job to sell, too, because we were having to fight all the other schools, because we were growing faster. ❞

Reng's staff did everything possible for the college "to pull away" from its three counterparts, according to Cameron. A-State went its own way in athletics. The school offered salaries to faculty that were higher than at the other institutions. ASC soon "got them thinking not [of] four agricultural schools but [of] two universities." By this latter statement Cameron meant the University of Arkansas in Fayetteville and the future "Arkansas State University."

An increased appropriation and abandonment of "lock-step" funding were vital if ambitious A-State officials were to vie with the University of Arkansas. Larger appropriations would offset a fundamental advantage of the older institution—land grant status. The Fayetteville campus received an income from extensive land holdings that the federal government granted to the State of Arkansas for this purpose in the nineteenth century. Arkansas State existed merely at the sufferance of the state legislature and waged a battle for funds every two years. Cameron reflected, "The land grant is kind of a magic word."

In the meantime, the campaign for formula appropriations for higher education continued in the legislature. As Cameron recalled, some of the committee meetings on this subject were "hectic," but eventually the bill passed:

66 I drafted a bill and gave it to a senator friend of mine in south Arkansas. I didn't want it to come from up here. They'd jump on it then. And he introduced it, and it passed, and they thought it was aimed at us. And he was from one of the other college towns. He and I became pretty good friends, and it passed, and we had our enrollment audited by hours and so forth by the legislative auditors. That way there wouldn't be any question about the enrollment. 99

Even with passage of this much sought-after legislation, the formula became fully effective only in 1957.

Though A-State labored under many handicaps and lagged far behind the University of Arkansas, the college possessed certain advantages. The college attracted most of its students from within a radius of 100 miles. Reng decided to publicize the benefits of the college within this "service area" and thus attract more students. A larger enrollment meant more state dollars under the new funding formula. Ray Hall remembered the day when the college executive summoned him and other officials to formulate plans for this recruitment program. Hall's field services division coordinated the effort:

66 President Reng called us in, and he said, 'Now, in building this school, we need numbers. Get numbers, but get good quality people.'. . . We didn't call it recruiting. We called it 'bringing in these high school graduates.' First map I made indicated that about ninety percent of our students lived within a 100-mile radius of Jonesboro. We began to call on our independent students and our three Greek sororities and our three Greek fraternities to assist us with this, making Arkansas State better known. Some groups on the campus that were of immense value to us were music groups like the Arkettes and the Arka Statesmen. We began to take those into the public schools throughout the area and before civic clubs. They gave fine programs. We made use of the FHA groups that came to the campus four times a year. Such groups as journalism day. . . . band days. A group downtown called the Jaycees volunteered to help us to make Arkansas State better known. I recall in '53, twenty-one or -two of those young men—on their own time and at their own expense—traveled throughout the area, went out over this part of the state visiting public schools and talking to their people in their civic groups, making Arkansas State better known in many of the outlying counties. 99

Hall recalled that A-State also hosted many functions on campus to publicize the school:

66 Then we organized certain on-campus situations like twirling clinics, the band camp, athletic clinics, ASU Rodeo by the agri boys, cheerleaders clinic. We called in some of our people and put on programs about four times a year. We called them senior days. We sent out invitations to people all over this area—the school people and the fathers and mothers and high school juniors and seniors—and asked them to come in. Of course, we provided them with literature and instructions. Attempted to make them better acquainted with the opportunities here on this campus. Teachers' meetings were

held throughout this area, so we invited those groups to the campus. We invited high school counselors, the superintendents' association, the principals' conferences. We invited many professional groups to meet on this campus. One especially good thing that we worked up, I thought, was what we called Legislative Day. It made us feel good when the representatives and senators and state officials came to spend a day on the campus to get better acquainted with what went on here. **"**

The new administration desired not only to cultivate community favor, but to impress upon the citizens of Jonesboro the financial importance of the college. The president and his publicity personnel went about both purposes with energy and conceived a unique stunt to set apart the monthly salaries of the faculty and staff from the income of other Jonesboroans. Reng described this unusual publicity tactic:

" We went to the bank and talked to them. . . . They brought a Brink's truck under guard out, and we paid the faculty in two dollar bills and, of course, they overflowed the cash registers downtown. There isn't any drawer for two dollar bills. They had them in shoe boxes and everything else. There was a lot of moaning and groaning about it. But it did make the town realize that there was a lot of people at the university spending money in town they didn't know, like janitors and maids and cooks and people like that. And even the students got in on the spirit. They'd go and cash their money and get two dollar bills and spread them around town. **"**

Ray Hall and his publicity agents represented a giant step in sophistication over the earlier, more modest efforts of the college to advertise its strengths. Sometimes these agents became a bit overzealous as they went about their duties. Donald Minx, who joined the faculty as director of bands in 1954, recalled that the college's publicity about him caused some embarrassment:

" All of a sudden, newspaper articles (before I've ever met my band) started hitting *The Jonesboro Sun,* and, man, you thought the

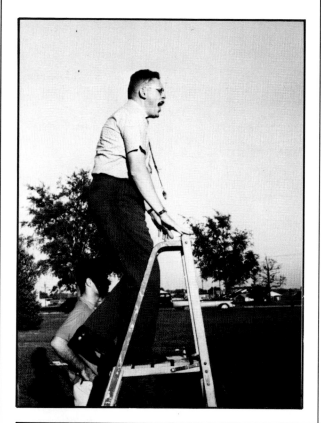

Donald R. Minx was a member of the faculty at A-State for 28 years and served most of the period as director of bands. He also served 17 years as chairman of the music department. Under his direction, the Marching Indians gained recognition as one of the finest musical groups in the Mid-South.

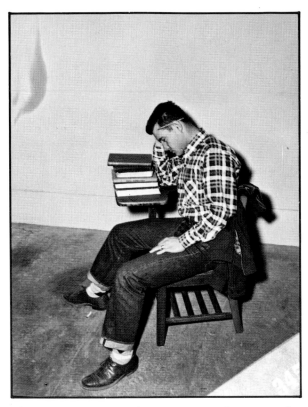

The curriculum apparently gave some students cause for unconscious meditation.

Carl Reng (left) and Linual Cameron, business manager of ASC, confer over coffee in the Wigwam.

Robert Ferralasco (center) was among the World War II veterans who attended ASC in the late 1940s. He became a faculty member in the next decade and later was appointed chairman of the information systems and business education department.

saviour had arrived all of a sudden. Suddenly, they're going to have a gassy marching band at the ballgames because some joker from Indiana is coming down, and he's got some clarinet player that was never in a marching band in his whole damn life as his assistant, and he's going to be here, and together they are going to put a marching band on the field. Well, it just got to the place that I woke up panicked, tight knots in the stomach and everything. I finally, one day, I called Ray Hall and I said, 'Hey, man, call off the dogs. You use one more article in the paper, and YOU are going to put the band on. I ain't about to.' 🎧

The desire to publicize the institution prompted the introduction of other programs in the 1950s. These innovations also had the purpose of strengthening the academic program and thus offering new career opportunities for the student body. The radio broadcasting program was one such innovation. The administration desired to employ the magic of radio waves as a means to become a part of every household within the school's service area. Charles Rasberry, who joined the radio staff in 1961, recalled that the station signed on the air on May 17, 1957, with a band concert:

🎧 We were using an old Western Electric transmitter, and the transmitter was in what had been a classroom. They had taken a classroom and put a wall in it, and on one side was a studio, and then the radio instructor-director's office was on the other side, and there was a little partition around that to separate it from the transmitter itself. And the control room, I recall, was in a closet that was adjacent to this room, and they had knocked a hole in that and put in a window so that you could see into the studio, but it was a closet. Then we had one other classroom which also had a partition in it, and we had a little teletype machine behind that. . . . We signed on with 760 watts of power. We had a little—what we called a one-bay antenna which was mounted atop Wilson Hall, and we covered I guess about ten to twelve miles with that 760 watts. 🎧

This decrepit and antiquated device seldom fulfilled its promise. Breakdowns plagued the broadcasters and were a sore spot with faithful listeners. To student broadcasters, regular programming and reliable transmissions were essential. Rasberry recalled that an embarrassing breakdown during the broadcast of a football game one Saturday afternoon finally led to getting something done:

🎧 The next Monday I remember Tex Plunkett going down with me to see Dr. Reng. And I said that we could teach radio to a certain extent without a radio station. [But] we are going to have to have a new transmitter because this one is done for. . . . A new transmitter would cost about $4,000. That was a lot of money in those days. I remember Dr. Reng saying, 'Well, let me talk to Mr. Cameron about it.' And apparently they talked later in the day because late that afternoon or the next afternoon, I remember Mr. Cameron stopping me in the hall, and [he] said, 'Go ahead and order the new transmitter.' I really think that was one of the most critical decisions that has ever been made in our program. 🎧

Broadcasting athletic events was a primary part of the radio station's duties, and the eventual formation of the Indian Radio Network constituted an important step for this program. Some doubts exist about the precise time of the creation of the network, but as Rasberry pointed out:

🎧 All admit that both KDRS in Paragould and KBTM in Jonesboro worked together and would originate broadcasts for themselves and for some of the other stations in the area. In those days, initially the games were carried by telephone lines to these other stations. Certainly Ted and Ray Poindexter and Paul Hoffman from those two stations have to be credited, I think, with the initial network operation. . . . Later then, when it appeared that we were going to have a radio department and when John Cramer came here, the idea was brought forward that, well, couldn't some of the new radio classes originate some of these games and feed them to KBTM and KDRS

and to Forrest City radio station and to Pocahontas radio station and other stations? It would give students a good opportunity for experience and at the same time reduce the costs of the radio station. They wouldn't have to send somebody over to do the games. So even before we had a station, some of our classes were originating these broadcasts on the Indian Network. 🎧

Within a short time, the station's call letters—KASU—became an important part of the listening audience's vocabulary. Rasberry related the origins of these letters:

🎧 Originally, we wanted the call letters KASC, but there was a school in Tempe, Arizona—Arizona State College—that had those call letters, KASC. So when application was made, we applied for KASU. Maybe somebody—maybe John Cramer or Carl Reng or Tex Plunkett, or somebody back in those days— [was] looking far enough ahead to think, well, maybe [university status is] coming down one of these years. So the call letters that we originally received were KASU. I have a letter in our files from Arizona State College. We hadn't been on the air very long with KASU when Arizona State got a bill through the legislature changing its name to Arizona State University. I had a letter in the files from some officials out there asking us if we would give up the call letters KASU now that they were a university since they understood we had originally been interested in KASC. They would be happy to give us their call letters. We said, 'No thanks, we will keep KASU.' 🎧

The marching band also served as an important publicity organ as well as an academic program. The band dated from the very early years of Aggie. However, the first formal band supported by the college appeared in 1947. With the arrival of Donald Minx in 1954, the music program continued to flourish. The colorful, uniformed marching band became a formidable publicity agent for the energetic college. Furthermore, a bachelor's degree in music education from Arkansas State soon became

Two long-time department chairmen are shown at a campus function: C.C. Carrothers of the business department (left) and Duane Haskell of the music department.

"essential" for young persons who desired to teach band in the public schools of the service area.

The beginnings of this new band were modest. Minx recalled his first halftime show with much dismay:

❝ Oh Lord, I will never forget the first ballgame we played for either. That was horrible. We got there and played the national anthem, and just as I stood up and gave the downbeat to the national anthem—this was down in the old Kays Stadium; it's gone now—somebody turned out the lights. Well, I didn't know that they had always used the lights out for the national anthem and put the light on the flag—nobody told me that. We hadn't memorized the national anthem, and I think they heard me yelling all the way downtown, 'Who in the hell turned out the lights?!' and 'Get your cigarette lighters out quick!' ❞

An appearance of the marching band during halftime of a football game became a favorite in the minds of many spectators. Minx reflected upon the reason for such expectations of the audience:

❝ I see the reason for the marching band at the football games to be a part of an entertainment package for the people that are coming to the college, the university, or the high school for a game, for an event of some type. . . . I don't mean to say that I don't think it can be an educational experience for the kids in the band and a learning thing, and certainly the coordination of the physical and the mental and the musical all do tie together and develop a great deal. But . . . I don't kid myself—I read a book recently, *The Aesthetic Value of the Marching Band,* and I thought, 'Well, bull.' ❞

Minx claimed the primary function of the marching band was to create a mood:

❝ Damn it, you get out there and you work your can off, and you do it because it is going to put something before the public that represents the institution for which you work and represents the area of your expertise at that institution, and that is the way I visualize the thing. I also see it . . . as being an awfully important thing, if it is handled right, as far as controlling mood, enthusiasm, and all that sort of thing. Get a band playing at the right time and the right spirited reaction to it, and I am sure that there has to be some sort of psychological effect upon the players out there. I used to play football myself, and I am not sure that you hear—that you listen to it, but maybe you sort of feel it or sense this sort of thing happening out there. I think the band is part of that . . . whether it be a basketball game or a football game. ❞

Among the annual musical events at A-State in this era, the Dixie Band Camp performed a valuable dual role as publicizer of the college and educational device for public school students. Although other colleges had sponsored this gathering in the past, this musical summer camp soon found a permanent home on the Jonesboro campus. Minx recalled that Scrubby Parker, director of bands in the Pine Bluff public schools, first proposed that ASC host this camp:

❝ He told me . . . he thought that Dixie Band Camp needed to move off the campus of Monticello A&M for various reasons, and if Arkansas State College would be interested in having it come to the campus, why didn't I write them a formal invitation and spell out facilities, what would be available, what they would be charged, all this sort of thing? . . . And I came back and talked with Mr. Cameron about it and talked to Dr. Reng about it and Dr. [Duane] Haskell, who was head of the music department at the time, and we set up what would be a reasonable charge for room and board and told them what facilities we would have and so forth. . . . And subsequently they accepted the invitation. ❞

Many years elapsed before the music program began to take on the proportions that Donald Minx desired. The music department began in very rustic quarters in the old music building (formerly a barn) located at the corner of Caraway and Aggie roads. Minx received a shock when he entered the premises in the summer of 1954:

The 1950s saw an end to the tradition of homecoming parades down Main Street in Jonesboro.

Stationary displays supplanted the homecoming parade as a sign of campus spirit. This fixed display (at far right) was a forerunner of today's elaborate structures.

" Gosh, I don't know what it had been. It certainly hadn't been a music building. It was a horrible, horrible hole. . . . I remember, you could go up about twenty-eight steps, and when you got to the top of the steps on the second floor and you could look down, and there was a crack that was fully five inches wide that went all the way to the bottom. You could see where the front end and the back end of the building was separating that way. Down on the first floor they showed me a room that had had the print shop in it. It had about eight pillars in it, an old dirt floor, and just an awful mess and said, 'Now, you draw up what you would like to have, and we will renovate this and make a band room out of it.' . . . So they were able to put in some I-beams and conceal four of the posts nicely and make enough room that we could rehearse, and a year or so later we had it, and it was a very adequate facility for what we had at that time in the way of a band. The acoustics were horrible in the whole building. Good Lord, you could hear anybody that sang in any room in it. "

Another element in efforts of the Reng administration to advertise was *The Herald,* the campus newspaper which served as an academic program and news disseminator. However, this journal soon began to reach beyond the borders of the campus. Spreading news is always a sensitive matter, and participants in the media often run a risk of encountering a hostile reader. Tex Plunkett, who was faculty advisor to *The Herald* staff, recalled the reaction of a south Arkansan to a student editorial:

" One morning Dr. Reng called me over to his office and said he had a problem. 'A state representative from south Arkansas is just raising hell over something he read in *The Herald.'* Dr. Reng said he didn't see anything wrong the way it read. He had the paper out and looking at it. I looked at it, and I saw what he was talking about. . . . It was an editorial written by a young man called Lee Adler, a fine young man. I believe when he went to church on Sunday . . . the preacher had preached on what a shame it was for businessmen to go to church on Sunday and then on Monday get out and cut each others' throats. So that's what Lee Adler had based his

editorial on. I didn't see anything wrong in it, so it ran in *The Herald.* This guy from south Arkansas got hold of it and wrote Dr. Reng and said if that is what they taught at the journalism department and Arkansas State about capitalism, then he was going to introduce a bill to bar the whole works. That was it. Nothing excites a college president more than [to] have a member of the legislature up in arms. "

The college executive placed responsibility for the matter in Plunkett's lap. *The Herald* sponsor continued:

" Dr. Reng asked me what to do about it. I told him I thought the best thing for him to do was to write him a letter and tell him that was just one student's opinion, and we appreciated him taking that much interest in *The Herald,* and if he would continue to read *The Herald,* that he would find an editorial that would have an opinion just almost opposite of that. Dr. Reng thought that was a good idea, and he wrote the letter, and I went back and told Lee that he had gotten us into a little bit of trouble, and he was a real nice lad and said he didn't mean to do anything like that. I told him to work on an editorial to rebut that, and we will run it in about three weeks. . . . About three weeks later he wrote another editorial and ran it in *The Herald* with another name on it. The guy from south Arkansas wrote back after he read it and said he thought it was great. "

The growing educational institution also was publicized through the Arkansas State College Museum. Public school children were especially delighted to observe the intriguing artifacts. Although the museum began before World War II as a project of the History Club, it suffered from lack of a full-time director for many years. In 1953, Jean Williams, professor of chemistry, took over this position in addition to her eighteen-hour teaching load. While she added to the collections, her academic duties prevented any regular hours for the museum. Elizabeth Wittlake recalled that when she and her family arrived in Jonesboro in May 1956, she was excited to learn that the college possessed such a prize attraction. "I went on up and I found it [in Wilson Hall]," she said.

But "that's all I did," since it was not open. Another visit in September was futile. "I had to wait until about October or November," said Wittlake, before the gallery was open.

This uncertain status of the museum improved considerably in 1959, when Eugene B. Wittlake, professor of botany, assumed the directorship. Elizabeth Wittlake, wife of the director, soon became curator of history.

The museum struggled to survive the fifties and was saved by a move to temporary quarters in the old science building in 1957. E.B. Wittlake (left) took over the direction of the museum two years later from Jean Rosser Williams (center). With them is one of Wittlake's student workers, Tommy Dicus. Student help has been used extensively in expanding the museum.

Although the salaries of the Wittlakes and their staff were minimal (the director continued to teach part-time in the biology department and the curator was a "volunteer"), this new and eager staff stretched the precious funds as far as possible. This was especially true in new acquisitions for the museum. Travel was essential to such a task, and the new director scouted the region thoroughly for archaeological and Indian relics, as well as wildlife specimens and other artifacts related to the area. While the college authorized Wittlake a mileage fee, he nonetheless was required to maintain a tight budget in his travels:

❝ We camped to save money, and then once a week, we would go to a motel . . . to get a bath and stay overnight. . . . I built a trailer, and we cooked out of the trailer—had a kitchen in it and everything. And so I thought I operated about as cheap as we could. . . . Other schools I ran across in the field . . . had big fancy trailers for their museums and all the conveniences of home. **❞**

In spite of such hindrances as meager budgets, the new director made significant strides toward the modernization of this very important asset to the college. The museum occupied new quarters in the basement of the library in 1964 and served as a resource for seventeen academic courses.

Every academic program sought ways to expand course offerings and to attract more students. The agriculture department—at one time the primary purpose of the institution—became an especially effective means to bring potential students on campus. Olen Nail assumed the position of head of the agriculture department in 1953 and began a period of energetic recruiting. He recalled:

❝ We used to furnish judges for almost every fair within a hundred miles. I think that's the limit they gave me. If it's over a hundred miles, don't send them. And we'd even send them to Missouri. Yeah, we judged fairs all over. And I think the College of Agriculture was the first college—or the first department at that

A part of the campus life routine was Thursday afternoon drill on the ROTC drill field, followed by the cleaning of weapons.

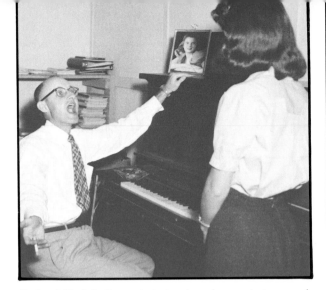

Richard K. Schall, music instructor, demonstrates vocal technique to one of his students.

John A. Galloway, who joined the faculty in 1948, instructed thousands of A-State students during his 36 years of service.

Edgar Kirk, former student and later an instructor in the history department, was popular among students and faculty for his wit and congeniality.

time—who brought in large bodies of students on judging day for many years and still do. Approximately 3,000 to 3,500 students brought on the campus once a year still. And we also have northeast Arkansas contests for parliamentary procedure and public speaking. **"**

The college also began to offer the prospects of graduate education in 1955. Perhaps these master's level courses benefited public school teachers most, since an advanced degree helped them to improve their skills and to earn better salaries.

The faculty of the college continued to offer an ever-widening variety of educational opportunities for students in the 1950s and 1960s, including the prospects of study abroad. This possibility was of unique benefit, since many of the young scholars were reared in a heavily rural environment where such opportunities seldom existed. Mildred Vance organized and escorted the first educational study tour of Europe in 1961. She led twenty-two eager travelers to nine nations over a period of five weeks.

Not all of the study tours went so smoothly, as Wanda Walker, a member of the English department, learned in one such overseas adventure. While her large group of thirty-five

students "was a congenial" one, this tour soon encountered "some headaches" when they arrived late in London for the return flight to the United States:

" They said, ' Oh well, you all are late, and we don't have any seats for you.' There I was with thirty-five people, and everybody was broke, nearly everybody. Well, it turned out that they did have seventeen seats. When that word became known, you should have seen those kids bolting, running over one another trying to get on that plane. Because as I said, they were all broke by that time. Well, we finally made it. They did take ten more of us on an Air India flight for the next day. They had ten seats available. The rest of us didn't know what was going to happen. But finally we got on the Air India flight in the first class section, which was quite an experience. That Air India is pretty plush, so it worked out pretty well for those of us who thought we were never going to get home. **"**

While the student body acquired access to broadening influences in the 1950s, the college administration maintained the traditional code of conduct. Chaperones regularly attended all social gatherings. These adult escorts were as a rule members of the faculty and staff. Paul and Lou

Couch routinely served in this capacity. "You know, back in those days you had to have chaperones," Lou Couch recalled. "The student body couldn't go anywhere without some faculty member with them." An individual student could not leave the campus without permission, and a faculty member was required to accompany any student group that departed the premises.

These guardians of the youths' morality watched for certain suspicious acts at dances, for instance. Paul Couch remembered that "we did everything but take a breath sample" in order to prevent the use of alcoholic beverages. "If you [a student] left in the middle of a dance, why, that was bad," said the former sponsor. Such an act was a telltale sign of base intentions. After an abrupt and unexplained exodus from the dance, "you had to account for yourself," added Lou Couch.

Dorm life continued to figure significantly in the students' existence at Arkansas State. Many faculty members had the dual responsibility of teaching and dorm manager—dorm "daddy" for the men, dorm "mother" for the girls. Gladys Hudgins, instructor in physical education, served in this capacity. While she agreed to the desirability of rules of conduct in the residence halls she also regarded some of the rules as excessive:

" Girls had to be fully dressed going across campus. They couldn't even wear their gym clothes across campus without having raincoats or something over them. And we always laughed at everybody, you know. Here on a sunny day you wear a raincoat to class. And, of course, the dorms closed at ten o'clock. And you were promptly standing there to lock the door when they came in and all that kind of thing. "

Each late arrival presented an excuse, some plausible, others ridiculous. "A train would . . . block them," recalled this dorm mother, was the most common explanation. The proximity of the railroad added some weight to the excuse, since there was no overpass close by.

Most of the problems that Hudgins and her colleagues in the dormitory system encountered were routine. Occasionally, though, a resident presented a bizarre case. Hudgins recalled:

" I had a young lady in the dorm that was as different from the ordinary student as daylight from dark. And, of course, there was a regulation that a person could not have a pistol in their possession in the dormitory. And she'd just likely be one place as another. We never got to bed very early, none of us. So one night about two o'clock in the morning someone knocked on the apartment door. And when I answered the door, she handed me the pistol pointed toward me. You can imagine how frightened I was. So when she saw I was so frightened, she turned it around and handed it to me and says, 'I just knew it was against the rules for me to have this in the dorm.' I won't forget that one. "

One of the continuing surprises at Arkansas State College in the 1950s and 1960s was the dramatic increase in enrollment. A limitless supply of students appeared to reside within the college's service area. A pull and push mechanism seemed to be at work. The administration's publicity efforts were paying dividends, but other forces were encouraging young Arkansans to attend institutions of higher education. The federal government played an important part in the growth of Arkansas State. Washington had been generous to the campus since the Depression era.

In 1945, the GI Bill of Rights contributed immensely to college enrollments and continued to do so for several decades. The most formidable federal incentive to higher education appeared in 1958 in the form of the National Defense Education Act, which made large scale loans available to needy students. This remarkable event, which occurred in President Dwight D. Eisenhower's administration, followed the surprising orbit of a Soviet satellite, Sputnik. Washington concluded that America's youth must acquire more and better college education in order for the United States to match this scientific feat. Robert Moore, dean of students, recalled that "everybody got scared" when Sputnik was launched:

" Man, we were going to lose out to the Russians because they put old Sputnik up there. And so the government put this money out, and nobody could get it but a science or a math [major] or a schoolteacher. And we got our first allotment of about $8,000 and started lending money. Well, it's gone from that till now when

we're in millions of dollars and all other kinds of work studies and grants and monies under the Basic Educational Opportunity Grants for where a very large percentage of the students now have some type of financial aid. "

Since the formation of Aggie in 1909, each president wisely selected the best qualified faculty possible. This often required employment of persons from other states. The absence of graduate programs in Arkansas' few colleges and universities seriously retarded this region. When an outsider made the decision to join the faculty at Arkansas State College, this determination was a big one. Few persons in neighboring states regarded Arkansas as "The Land of Opportunity" in spite of the boast on license plates. Donald Minx recalled his first reaction to the proposal of a friend that he look into the position of band director in 1954. "Oh, hell, that is the bowels of the earth," he scoffed. Although he had never visited the state before, he immediately thought of "swamps and rice and mosquitoes." "Thanks," he told his friend, "but forget it."

The growth of the student body was responsible for an increase in mandatory ROTC participation.

The fifties saw a growing enrollment on the A-State campus, along with an increase in the sale of freshman beanies.

Despite the major growth of the campus after World War II, the close rapport between faculty and students remained a vital part of campus life. This Modern Language Club picnic behind the Pasmore's home was an annual event.

When this friend admonished Minx for overlooking a good opportunity, the reluctant band teacher decided to make the trip from Indiana to Arkansas:

66 So we arranged the trip down here simply because I was told they would pay my expenses down and back and have an expense paid vacation in Arkansas. . . . Dr. Haskell was the chairman of the music department or division as it was called then at the time, and that was in 1954—Easter time—and I looked the campus over, looked the equipment over, met Dr. Reng, and talked with him at great length. When he got done interviewing me, why, I remember that I pulled out my book and started down my questions that I had for him then, and the nice thing about it was that I was completely relaxed because I didn't want the job. I was just down here for enjoying it. 99

After exhausting his long list of objections to residence in Arkansas, Minx surprisingly accepted the job! He explained this contradictory decision:

66 Dr. Reng impressed me so favorably that I decided . . . I could work with a man who was that positive. And he didn't hide anything and pussyfoot around anything and would come out and tell you what he stood for, whether you agreed with it or not. By gosh, you always knew. 99

In spite of the fact they had to go elsewhere to obtain an advanced degree, one of the steadiest suppliers of faculty for Arkansas State College was the student body. Elmer Mayes, whose career was interrupted by World War II, returned to finish his degree and joined the staff in 1957. A call from W.W. Nedrow, head of the science department, surprised Mayes. When Nedrow asked the former student to come to work for the college, Mayes immediately thought that Nedrow desired him to teach at the Beebe Branch, which ASC had recently acquired. Nedrow replied, "No, no, I want you to teach here." After some hesitation, Mayes accepted the position.

Marshall Matthews returned to his old college in 1955. Although he resigned a school superintendency to join the mathematics department, he did not regret the decision:

66 I suppose that they were looking for math teachers. They couldn't find any qualified teachers. I can imagine Dean Ellis . . . my old teacher, told Dr. Reng that I could do the job if he could get me. That's all that I can imagine. I know that one night I came down here to a homecoming dinner, and Dr. Reng left the dinner as he usually did a little early and came to my chair and said, 'I want to talk to you when you come into the football game.' I couldn't imagine what he wanted. I walked in, and he said, 'Marshall, you are going to come down here and go to work for us next Monday morning.' I said, 'I'm not so sure of that.' I said, 'I'll make up my mind until Wednesday.' . . . I went home and got to thinking about it and had three children to go to college, and I thought it would be worth it, if I'd come down here, to have them eat under my own table there for awhile. I'll save some money and be with the kids, enjoy Arkansas State again. 99

The faculty continued to produce unique personalities, although one of the longtime standouts, F.W. Plunkett, retired in 1953. Dean B. Ellis continued in service until 1965. But few academics possessed the unusual personal characteristics of Pat White, chairman of the English department. A scholar in the field of literature, he was a master of profanity. A compassionate person with the interest of students at heart, he often astounded his friends with brashness and bluntness. Wanda Walker knew him well:

66 He was a character. You could hear Pat almost anywhere on this campus when he was there in the office yelling at somebody. He was very outspoken. . . . He could get rough if he had to be rough—you know, he really had to tell somebody off. He didn't mince words. He could cuss like a sailor on occasion. He was a very humane person. He was a gentleman. I sometimes would shake my finger in Pat's face to straighten him out because, you see, he and I

had sat side by side during part of our graduate work up at the University of Arkansas. I had a little edge on some of the other teachers. 99

Most faculty members were quiet, efficient, and conscientious in performing their duties. Homer C. "Doc" Huitt fit this category completely—and then some. Huitt became chairman of the Department of History and Social Sciences in 1937. He retired in 1965, after a serious fall partially incapacitated him. A longtime member of this department, John Galloway, recalled this gentleman and scholar:

66 Dr. Huitt was a very splendid human being. He was a very kind person, a very friendly and outgoing, extremely energetic, and I think a very good department chairman. He had some peculiarities, shall I say? He spoke so rapidly that it was a little difficult at times to understand. He tended to be negligent at times in getting in reports and doing other things that he was asked to do as chairman, but there were many instances in which he helped other members of the department by going to bat for them when any kind of tough situation arose, and he had very strong support from members of the department. He was very friendly, not only with other faculty members but with students. He was an extremely moral individual, a man of very high principles, and I think a very good teacher. Some thought he was perhaps a little too lenient in grading. This perhaps was true, but I think he had a lot to offer people in his classes. On the whole, I think he was quite capable. 99

To perform their many duties in the 1950s and 1960s, the academic community expended much time and energy. Classes were very large with as many as eighty to 100 students per class. Many performed additional tasks such as teaching extension courses out of town, chaperoning, sponsoring social groups and honorary societies, and working in dormitories. Olen P. Nail, chairman of the agriculture department, discussed the problem of heavy teaching loads:

The registration process moved efficiently under the direction of N.D. Hazelbaker, chief academic officer.

Students continued to earn their college fees by providing much-needed labor during the fifties.

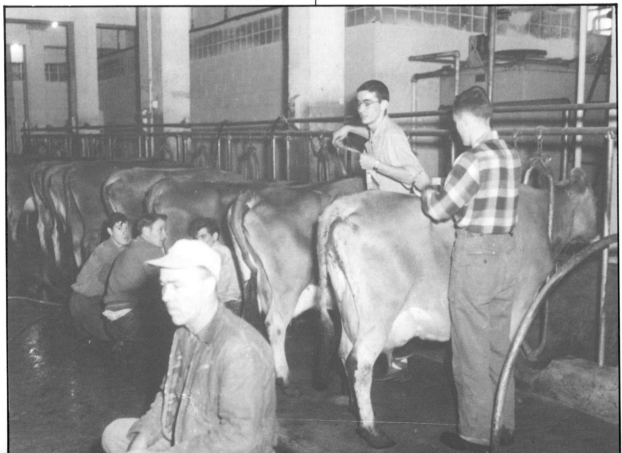

66 The average teaching load at Arkansas State at that time [early 1950s] was eighteen semester hours for teachers. . . . If they advised twenty students or more, then they cut that to fifteen. . . . The first few years after I came here I taught all the professional education and vocational education—about nine hours a semester—supervised as many as twenty-eight or twenty-nine practice teachers in vocational agriculture, and [was] department chairman, and had responsibility for the farm. I didn't have much time left over. . . . A lot of other faculty members and department chairmen had about similar loads. Everybody was heavy loaded because even with about 1,350 students, the faculty at Arkansas State was very, very small. 99

As the enrollment increased in the 1950s and 1960s, the faculty grew in proportion. In 1948 the college employed sixty-nine members with an additional twelve teachers in the training school. This high school was discontinued in 1954. By 1958 the college faculty roster listed 104 members. The figure continued to increase. By 1966, forty percent of these persons held the doctorate, an essential degree for an institution with university aspirations.

The faculty constituted a corporate body that maintained a life of its own, one seldom seen by the public. These career servants of higher education continually sought to improve their condition on the college campus. They desired more equitable working conditions, better personal and family security, and the opportunity to improve their professional skills. However, the Arkansas Teachers' Retirement System, which included both public school and college teachers, lacked flexibility. For instance, the benefits of this system could not be transferred out of state. Linual Cameron, the A-State finance officer, participated in an effort to persuade the state legislature to permit college faculties to participate in Social Security as a secondary form of retirement in 1956. When the bill came up for debate, Cameron concluded that the public school lobby was certain to defeat the measure if the legislature did not vote on the bill immediately. He recalled:

" I said, 'Dr. Reng, go back there and get the Speaker of the House to call the bill up as soon as we can. If we don't call it this morning, we can't pass it this afternoon because they're taking the votes off of this bill as fast as they can.' He went around and called the Speaker of the House out and got him to call up the bill, and we passed it. "

Other benefits the faculty acquired in the 1950s included a health and life insurance program. Like most innovations on campus, the group insurance program cost money. Cameron recalled that the decision to contribute to Social Security delayed the possibility of funding the insurance package:

" But two or three years later, I said to him [Reng], 'Well, we're ready now. I think we got enough money. We're going to look at a health program.' . . . We got the [faculty] committee together, and they came up with an insurance program. "

Many faculty members lamented the absence of a leave program to enable them to earn a doctorate or to perform advanced study. Although a few academics returned to graduate school at their own expense, the cost of maintaining families and an education was excessive. John Galloway remembered his experience while on leave to the University of Missouri (without pay) and was pleased when he and Robert Ferralasco had the opportunity to draw up a leave program:

" We gathered some information from a few other institutions and drew up a plan, and in consultation with President Reng worked out a program which was finally approved by the board of trustees and was soon put into effect so that once the trustees were in the position to put some money into the program, we were able to grant leaves of absence for semesters or for entire years or for summer terms. At first, this was used primarily to help those who wanted to go back to school and work on their terminal degrees but has more recently been expanded to include more persons with terminal degrees who

have a need for time off to engage in research and writing activities. "

Even within a body that lauded equality and collegiality, not all faculty members at Arkansas State were treated equally. Female members of the academic community were keenly aware of inequities. Male colleagues often looked upon them much as men then viewed female public schoolteachers. The women were merely supplementing the family income. Wanda Walker of the English department felt this inequity when she assisted her chairman with a special project during her off-time in the summer. The administration assured her that she would receive a good increase on her next contract. When this raise failed to materialize, she inquired:

" I got $200 in comparison to a $1,000 raise that a lot of people were getting. So I said something to Dr. [Alfred E.] Leja [department head] about it, and he said, 'Oh, Wanda, I'm still working on that.' He and Bob Martin [the dean] both went back, and they were told, 'She doesn't need any more raise. She has a husband.' "

Gladys Hudgins confirmed this situation when she declared that "it was very difficult for a woman to get . . . a fair shake salary-wise." She recalled that one departmental administrator informed her that "it wasn't necessary for the woman to earn the money because after all the women didn't earn a living."

In 1954, an Arkansas State College Faculty Club was organized for the betterment of the academic community. Three years later this organization became the Faculty Association. A Faculty Council (now the Senate) consisted of members elected from the Faculty Association and spoke for the entire body. Wanda Walker participated in the pioneering efforts of this group to elevate the consciousness of the faculty and to acquire a greater voice on the campus. She recalled that in the 1950s and early 1960s, "We were concerned because the faculty really was sometimes treated as stepchildren, not children but stepchildren." As the council went about this mission for the faculty, Walker recalled "a few hassles" with the administration. When the

The library in the basement of Wilson Hall served thousands of ASC students, but was inadequate for the needs of a university.

council drafted a segment of a report for the North Central Association of Colleges and Schools, the administration concluded that this item did not represent the best interest of the college. She recalled, "We got looked right straight in the eye and told what we were going to put in that new study."

For many years the administration had consisted of only a few individuals, with the president exercising a close, personal control over the institution. It had not been uncommon for V.C. Kays to engage in some task in every area of campus affairs in one day. By the 1950s the term "administration" began to take on a more impersonal meaning. It consisted of not just the chief executive officer but lesser officials, each assisted by a growing clerical staff, and each offical directing a specialized task: academics, student affairs, athletics, finance, housing, or maintenance.

In this atmosphere of growing impersonality, the faculty often received written directives from a superior and more distant administrator, whereas in the past the assignment might have been delivered verbally. Sometimes these instructions reflected the growing distance between superiors and subordinates. Wanda Walker recalled one written directive that caused a pained expression on many faces. Faculty members were to ensure at the end of the day that all venetian blinds were lowered and closed. When a member of the history department failed to fulfill these orders, she soon heard from someone above, Walker related:

❝ Over in the education building . . . there's a little room that's way up at the top—just an isolated little room up above the second floor of the building. So a teacher in the history department once had her office over there in that little room. Well, she figured that nobody was looking way up there at those windows. She got a call one time from one of the administrative offices saying, 'I want you to adjust those shades. Quit leaving that place so messy.' ❞

Occasionally, a directive from mysterious sources was impossible to execute and provoked a good laugh. According to Walker:

The ever-present lines grew even longer as the student body passed the 3,000 mark in the late 1950s.

❝ Another time we got a directive from one of the administrative officers telling us how to wear our academic attire. He said, 'Wear your cap, your mortar board, straight on your head with the tassle on the left side over the right eye.' We never did quite figure out how that was to be pulled off. ❞

Administrative positions were places of much responsibility, and faculty members routinely sought them as a method of advancement. These posts required an attitude of detachment, compassion, and conscientious devotion to the general welfare. As finance officer of the college, Linual Cameron encountered many instances that required him to say no to the demands of subordinates. At other times, he was in a position to assist some departments. When the chairman of the history department failed to request the addition of a teaching slot during a period of rapid growth, Cameron recalled, "I said, 'Man, I know enough about history [the department]. . . that he needs it,' so I added some [funds] to his budget." In another instance, the finance officer materially aided the sciences:

❝ The high schools had a better program—I mean equipment—than [our] school did. That was bad to me. I remember adding, I forget how many thousands of dollars that I added to the science budget down there one time to buy equipment. . . . The federal government was . . . putting a lot of money into high school science. They were putting a bunch of money in there. Well, they were not giving us any money, and those science departments out there—they had better science equipment than we had here in the college, which was bad. We train teachers, and we had inferior equipment in the science department then. ❞

Occasionally, a faculty member ran afoul of the administration and received a surprise summons to the president's office. One such individual was Bernard Gorrow, a member of the history department. Gorrow took his meals in the college cafeteria, since his family resided in Memphis. At that time, this facility was located in the basement of Commons Building (now the College of Nursing and Health Professions). As many patrons of a common eating establishment

As fraternities and sororities grew in size and number, they became more important sources of campus entertainment.

The pomp and ceremony associated with academic tradition are always observed at graduation exercises. Baccalaureate services also were a traditional part of graduation exercises until the early sixties.

will do, Gorrow innocently complained one morning about the small helping of pancakes and asked for more. When a server replied rather abruptly, Gorrow responded that (in the words of Edgar Kirk to whom he related the story) "he was going to write Mr. Goodyear and tell him . . . he could come down here and find a recipe for making rubber that beat anything he had." This offhand remark led to an unexpected event. In a short while Gorrow received a summons to the president's office. As Kirk recalled him telling:

**&& On the way over there he thought, 'What have I said to some of these students here in the Bible Belt? Then a thought occurred to me,' he said, 'as I was going over there. I wonder if that man would be foolish enough to ask me to head this social science department for the remainder of the semester while Dr. Starr is gone?' Gorrow said, 'I began to think of all of the various excuses that I could put up for not doing so. I just simply didn't want it. Lo and behold, I walked in that office, and he looked up at me.

He said, 'What's this I hear about you criticizing the pancakes in the cafeteria?' Gorrow said, 'I was so shocked, stricken, and so disgusted that I came right back to my office and took the letter from my desk that I had been holding for several days from Idaho State University offering me a job in the sociology department. I put that letter in my pocket and carried it home that night and wrote my letter of acceptance.' 55**

Many such incidents were a product of the growing pains of the college, which passed the 3,000 mark in enrollment in 1960. This was a far cry from the mere 863 in 1951. The number of students continued to increase dramatically in the 1960s. Within the administration, the faculty, the student body, and other areas of the campus, new responsibilites and new problems were arising with remarkable frequency.

In spite of these stresses and the short tempers such problems sometimes provoked, a feeling of community prevailed over the differences of opinion. Members of the college community regularly gathered in the Wigwam to fraternize, drink a cup of coffee, and exchange news about the latest developments on campus or in Little Rock (the cornucopia, the place where the money was). Even Reng found time in his busy routine to join the crowd. Robert Ferralasco, a former student and then instructor in business, remembered the camaraderie with fondness:

66 We all drank coffee and ate doughnuts together down in the Wigwam in the basement of Wilson. We decided we'd sit at the various tables and discuss things, and the president was very good about coming down and spending a lot of time with the faculty discussing the problems of the day. You could ask questions, and he usually came up with what you wanted to hear. Well, maybe not what you wanted to hear, but what he was going to do about solving the problem. 99

Phil Bridger, now director of housing, looked forward in his student days to joining his classmates in front of the Wigwam's jukebox:

66 You went over to the old Wigwam, and you knew everybody. Why, you couldn't wait to get out of class to get over there. You know, that was the place. Summertime you went over there, and you danced by the jukebox. . . . It just had a lot of togetherness and meant a whole lot. I think that's one thing that I don't know if anybody has it now. 99

The pleasure derived from this mingling enabled the clientele to ignore the Wigwam's crowded and sometimes unsanitary conditions. Donald Minx was surprised one day when John Rauth, instructor in the physical education department and coach, suddenly let out an oath. Minx related:

66 Gosh, I still remember the day I was sitting down there with John Rauth having a cup of coffee, and he suddenly exploded. I looked down in the bottom of his cup, and there was coffee, of course. You never threw anything out in those days. The coffee had been served the day before, and there was a great big old cockroach down in the bottom of the dang thing. You can imagine

John Rauth and what he had to say about that. That was pretty colorful. 99

Annual faculty events brought together the entire academic community including wives and children. The Christmas banquet was the climactic get-together of the year. Mildred Vance characterized the event as "a family situation":

66 We had the Faculty Women's Club sponsor the Christmas dinner, but all the children came. Now . . . most of the faculty children attended the demonstration school. So they did the entertaining for the faculty. But it was kind of a nice thing in that, you know, it really was a family situation. Faculty and children, and there was a lot of concern and real deep love and understanding, I think, for each other in those early days. 99

Perhaps this closeness of the college community accounted for the steadiness and balance with which Arkansas State College managed one of the most explosive social crises of the 1950s and 1960s—integration. A remarkable change had occurred in the black community of the state and the nation since World War II. Blacks were much more aware of their potential power at the polls and had acquired new confidence as well as wealth in the course of their service in the armed forces and in war industries. With these experiences behind them, blacks were determined to reject the Jim Crow law that offered but failed to deliver "separate but equal" educational facilities.

The athletic department was established as an entity separate from the physical education department in 1959. The Chief Big Track tradition of a triumphant ride across the field after a touchdown also began that year.

From fads to sophisticated arts, the campus reflected national collegiate trends. Students participated in dramatic arts productions, musical groups such as Bill Bell and the Tribe, tonsorial exercises, and skit nights.

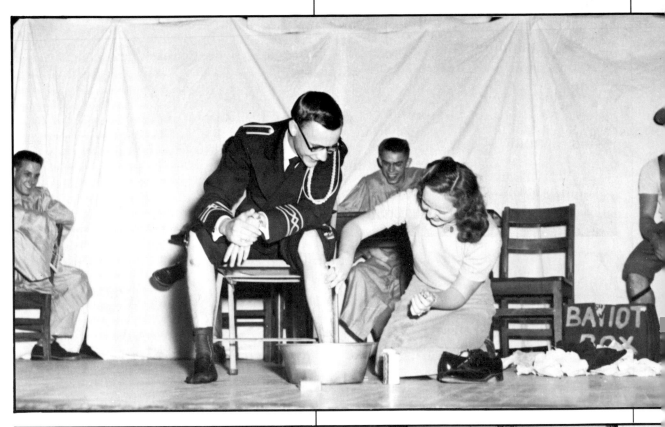

Some members of the Jonesboro black community attempted to enroll at Arkansas State College in the early 1950s, but were unsuccessful. These persons were schoolteachers who desired to return for additional course work or for a master's degree under a cooperative program with the University of Arkansas. The actual decision to integrate A-State was not made by campus authorities but by the United States Supreme Court. In Brown vs. Board of Education of Topeka in 1954, the highest court of the land rejected "separate but equal" facilities as "inherently unequal." When the attorney general of Arkansas, in turn, declared that this ruling applied to institutions of higher education within the state, Arkansas State College was constrained to comply with the law.

Once the decision to integrate had been made, college authorities proceeded cautiously but firmly to carry out this momentous legal decision. President Reng and his subordinates realized that A-State was in the public eye, since the University of Arkansas at Fayetteville had admitted black students several years earlier. Reng explained the procedure he employed to bring the first black students onto the college grounds:

❝ So we decided we were going to take one or two, but we wanted to be sure they were going to be real topnotch kids. A man by the name of Mr. Johnson ran a grocery store over in the colored section of town, and everybody was indebted to him—the colored people. They loved him. We went to Mr. Johnson and talked to him. Said, 'We'd like to take a couple of youngsters, but we want them to be good ones to start with.' He said, 'I'll pick you out two.' And he picked out two. So we enrolled them a week before school started. We said, 'We don't want you to come to class for the first week. Just don't come.' The newspapers were on us. They were saying, 'You got any here?' I said, 'I haven't seen any. I haven't seen any.' About a week after school started, we told them to go to class. They went to class. You didn't hear a thing about it. The newspapers didn't even pick it up. **❞**

117

Actually, three blacks were enrolled during that first year: Walter Strong, Fred Turner, and Larry Williams. Strong, who had graduated from high school in Turrell, Arkansas, was a veteran who sincerely desired to continue his education. In 1955 he was working for two Jonesboro businesses. Strong related a story about their assistance:

66 I told Frank [Angelo] that I was going to leave him, and I never will forget. . . . He says, 'Where are you going, Chicago or Detroit?' And I told him no, I was going to college. He said, 'Well, why don't you go to Arkansas State in light of the recent Supreme Court ruling?' My statement to him was that I hadn't thought about it. I don't want to create any ruckus or anything of the kind. I want an education. From that point, he told me that he knew Dr. Reng and he'd talk to Dr. Reng. . . . At the same time, I was working full-time with him, but I was working part-time as a janitor for Porter's Typewriter, and on weekends I would go out and clean up Mrs. Porter's house for her. I told her that I was thinking about going to school. So she said, 'I know Dean Hazelbaker personally,' and she called Dean [N.D.] Hazelbaker one Saturday afternoon, and they made an appointment for me the following Saturday. 99

Many misconceptions have occurred about the steps by which these first blacks were admitted to Arkansas State College. Some whites have alleged that the black community—through the National Association for the Advancement of Colored People (NAACP)—conspired to gain them admittance. However, the college administration revealed a readiness to admit them. After clarifying the state attorney general's ruling, Reng telephoned Walter Strong to inform him that he could enroll. A few days later the president held a conference with Strong to iron out details of registration. Strong recalled this meeting:

66 We would be accepted in toto, and he went on to mention that he was going to prepare his staff and that he was not going to take any mess off of them, and that it was possible that we could have some trouble, but he wanted us to

know—wanted me to know—that he would be behind us 100 percent. He also asked me, did I know the other two boys, Larry and Fred, and I told him I did know both of them. And he said at that point that he would probably think that I would be leader since I was older and had been in the military and all and asked me if I would get in touch with them. 99

College officials carefully prepared the faculty for the presence of the black students in their classes. Wanda Walker recalled that Reng and the academic dean met with the Faculty Council and discussed the faculty members most likely to be receptive to the new students. Although she recollected that this gathering "picked the teachers," these designees could refuse if they wished. Within each department, the administration polled faculty opinion about the presence of blacks in their classes. Edgar Kirk recalled that the procedure in the history department went smoothly:

66 Our chairman called us together that fall and told us that some, as we said then, 'colored people' were going to enter, and if we objected . . . to any black being in our class, let it be known. 'You let me know, and they'll not be put in your class, and there will be nothing said or done about it.' There was one person in the social science department who said, 'I'd rather not have one.' I don't recall. I don't believe that I got one that semester. In fact, I sort of wished that they would give me one. I wanted the experience, but I don't recall that I got one for a semester or two. 99

On September 12, 1955, following a separate registration process, Walter Strong and his two classmates reported for their first classes. As the senior of the three recalled, the white students were somewhat tense upon his arrival in the first class session, but they soon relaxed. His second session went more smoothly. He reported:

66 The second class that I attended—I never will forget the day I don't believe—was a history class, again in the educational building at one o'clock, and just the preclass chatter's going on,

The pep rally remained a vital part of the campus scene.

and I walked into the room, and all of a sudden everybody got quiet. And a fellow named Joel Breeding [was] sitting at the back, and he looked around. . . . He broke the silence with 'Oh, hello there, come on in and sit down.' So that broke that, and then later on the next class was a biology class, and a similar thing happened with a fellow by the name of Womack. . . . From that time on we had very little or no trouble. **"**

This favorable reception of Strong and his two classmates was not out of character. Generally, the college community went about its routine as though nothing exceptional had just taken place. Phil Bridger was present on campus in 1955 and noted the unruffled behavior of the student body:

" Somebody had to tell us to know if it was integration. It was no problem. Of course they were—they fit right in. . . . I can't remember any abuse being shown about it. I think a lot of people might have talked about it, but most of the students—I can't remember it being even any kind of a problem one way or another. **"**

For such a momentous event to occur so quietly was testimony to the solid, good sense of the members of the college community. Reng recalled an event that took place a few months after integration that illustrated the quiet nature of this movement at State College:

" An interesting thing [occurred] about six months later—some guy from Missouri was down, and he said, 'One thing I like about this school is you don't have any coloreds.' I said, 'Well!' He said, 'My daughter is down here, and we're proud.' I knew dang well his daughter was in class with one of them, and she hadn't told her dad. So I didn't tell him either. **"**

Considerable pressure rested upon Reng and his associates, since journalists prowled the campus for news and reported it fully. Edgar Kirk wondered about the conduct of the administration, but concluded that generally the process went "very smoothly":

Basketball fans in the 1960s got their money's worth. Jerry Rook, the most prolific scorer in ASU's basketball history, was followed by John Dickson, the Indians' second most prolific scorer and best all-time rebounder. The experienced Rook (right) assists freshman teammate Dickson prior to the 1963-64 season.

George Glenn, rushing to beat out a bunt, brought recognition to the Arkansas State University baseball program in the 1960s as a three-time All-America selection.

119

> The newspaper . . . in Little Rock got word that we were going to integrate. They sent reporters here. The administration dodged them and gave them no information and got some criticism for not having any information. Any time they would ask to see somebody he would be out of the office, or he would be where he could not be contacted, and they got some criticism for that. But the integration went quite smoothly considering some of the furor that had been created in some of the other situations over the state or in the South in general. We never had any problem that I know of with integration here. It was done quietly and, as they thought in those days, discreetly. We wonder today with the atmosphere as it is why they had gone to the trouble to handle it as they did, but they were handling it in a different situation than what we are in today. "

A spirit of cooperation characterized all parties to this remarkable event. Reng fulfilled his promise to support the blacks, and when he desired their assistance, these new students kept their part of the bargain. The first test of this agreement took place when an anonymous caller threatened Fred Turner. Walter Strong related:

> Fred did get a threat. Fred's mother was a schoolteacher, and I think they thought Fred initiated the action, and maybe his mother was responsible for it. So he did get a threat once and called me that morning before he came out. He didn't particularly want to come to school. I told [him], 'Come and we'll go and talk to Dr. Reng about the case.' So we did, and as I understand it . . . Dr. Reng called the chief of police, and they did patrol Fred's house because it was just his mother and him living in the house. "

The blacks reciprocated when the A-State choir scheduled a concert in Memphis. Since one black sang in the aggregation, Reng feared an incident:

> We always went to Memphis about twice a year and broadcast. I just knew that with that [black] boy in the choir, the old boys over in eastern Arkansas sitting in a rocking chair [were]

going to throw a fit. So I called the boy, and I said, 'You'd do us a great favor if you just didn't show up.' He said, 'Okay.' I mean they cooperated all the way. The choir sang, and he wasn't there. And so we had fine cooperation from them. From then on it was no problem, of course. It was just that first break that everybody was making a big to-do about. "

The former president applauded all three of these pathbreaking young men: "They were real fine young men."

As the pressure of those first days of integration eased, an air of relaxation began to sweep the campus. In such an atmosphere inadvertent errors often occur, mistakes that evoke a hearty laugh, and everyone exults because they know a victory has been won. Walter Strong and his friends enjoyed a good laugh on Robert Moore, dean of students, a short time after the crisis had passed. Even though the dean had informed Strong that, as a Mississippian, he did not approve of integration, this college official accepted and enforced the controversial law. Strong described the chuckle on Moore:

> We were sitting around in the general assembly dispersed and all, and Dean Moore finished his persuasion talk, and he said, 'We all in here are free, white Americans, and I can't tell nobody how to vote.' The student body cracked up. Then he said, 'Okay, I made a mistake. Go ahead and get your laugh out.' So we had some real good times. "

The athletic teams soon reflected this important step toward equality of the races. Ike Tomlinson, a former director of athletics, recalled that segregation had been an embarrassment among athletes in this region for many years and that little or no difficulty occurred when the new policy took effect:

> Many teams came in prior to that time, particularly baseball from the North, who would have colored boys, and we were not allowed by state law to take them into the dining hall to feed them or house them in the dormitory. If they

came, I had to go get them a room at one of the motels, whichever one would take them. Many times we had to carry their food out from the cafeteria, and they sat in their bus and ate it, and I know we were criticized by our own faculty people about bringing people here and treating them like that. But our hands were tied because it was a state law. Yet suddenly that changes in 1955, and a [black] boy plays—and no incident [occurs]. We had a natural fear of what might happen. You have a basketball arena full of people and a very explosive issue like that, and here the team brings out two colored boys. We were supposed to be living in a very volatile community, and yet we had no problems of that kind. I'm very thankful for that. "

Such issues as integration did not retard the progress of Arkansas State College in other areas. The athletic program made considerable progress, although the coaching staff labored under many handicaps. A-State was a relatively unknown, often ridiculed, and sometimes ignored college in the state in the early 1950s. Its budget was meager. Yet the coaching staff accomplished many things, while instructing physical education classes as part of their duties.

Perhaps the most pressing problem was the inadequate budget. Tomlinson wrestled mightily with this problem but never fully overcame such stringencies. Linual Cameron laughed as he recalled the deviousness of the athletic director, who employed many ruses to obtain more money:

> The athletic department was one of our big problems. I look back on that and laugh and kid some of them on the things they did. Like Ike loved baseball—Ike Tomlinson loved baseball. I think the world and all of Ike. I did then, but he worked every scheme possible he could to get money for baseball. Such as he would say so and so is going to give him the lumber if he could make a dugout. Well, he conned me—Ike Tomlinson conned me more than anybody else. Well, come to find out this lumber he had was old beat up lumber—wasn't worth a dime. And I had committed and had to go ahead with it. "

Once Tomlinson proposed to Cameron that they turn a portion of a college farm at Walcott into a golf course. The college "can make some money," the athletic director said convincingly. Cameron replied, "Are you sure?" "Oh, yeah, we'll use students to keep it up." Much to Cameron's disgust, the new course attracted so few paying customers that "we never even paid for the mowing." The finance officer informed the president about the losing proposition and suggested that—without telling Tomlinson—the college should turn the new golf course into pastureland. This project was "costing us too much money." Reng agreed, but urged that the cows be turned in quickly "before Ike gets up there and sees it." Cameron was ecstatic. Tomlinson, the "con artist," had had the tables turned on him. Cameron recalled, "I laughed at that until I couldn't breathe!"

Of course, the star of the athletic program in the early 1950s was Frosty England, head football coach. Like Tomlinson, England fretted about the absence of funding and facilities. Although he obtained thirty-five full scholarships, these were totally inadequate. He could hardly attract the most proficient players, but attempted to stretch these benefits as widely as possible:

❝ Now a scholarship was considered to be . . . their housing, their meals, and their fees. Their books I had to provide by hook or crook or bargain, borrowing, begging, and asking graduates to please sell me theirs cheap. And I'd keep them. I ran a little library in my office of used books and so forth from one year to the other. And I would take those scholarships—your best players, I'd have to give them what we had as a full scholarship. But amongst a large number of them till they could prove themselves of good quality I'd break that down. Maybe one boy would get his housing and one meal a day. Another boy might get two meals a day. **❞**

Quarters for the squad left much to be desired, when competing schools housed their players in new, first-class dormitories. According to England:

The band, cheerleaders, majorettes, and football team of 1960 are represented by this quartet of Larry Manness, Carol Carr, Mary Mahfouz, and Roy Nelson.

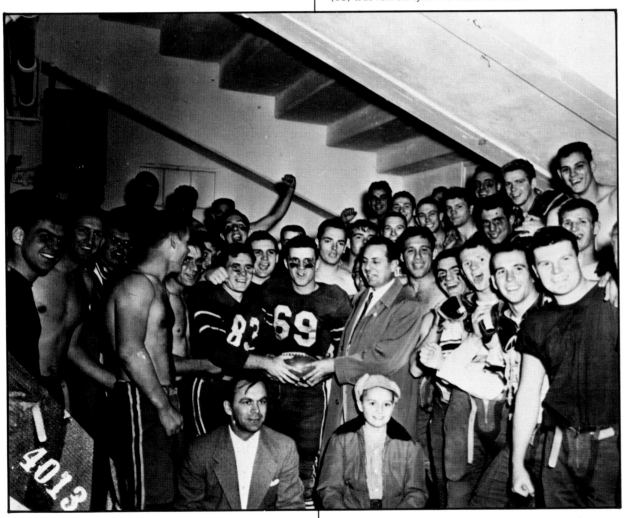

Jubilant Indians celebrate their victory over Memphis State in 1953. The win, under the coaching leadership of Frosty England (center right), was the highlight of the football team's first undefeated season since 1915. Richie Woit (center left), three-time All-American and Most Valuable Player in the Mid-Bracket All-American team, later signed with the Detroit Lions. His jersey number (83) was retired after the 1953 season.

❝ My housing was in the loft of an old dairy barn that stood near the present site of the post office on the campus. And we scrubbed and cleaned and partitioned a loft, which was a large loft for a barn, into housing there. And then I had some housing above the swimming pool in the old gymnasium. Had Army cots in there—dormitory style, no rooms. Had about thirty or forty cots in that area. And one year I know I had some housing in the second floor of what they called the hangar in those days. But those things made my recruiting difficult because, though these boys didn't grow up in luxury, they'd certainly been used to better housing than I could show them when they came here. So it was commonly referred to as the 'pig pen,' where our boys lived. And I lost some good players because I couldn't compete. **❞**

Residing in the athletic apartments in the old dairy barn left indelible impressions upon the occupants. Bill Davidson recalled the year that he and his wife, Jean, stayed there:

❝ I mean the horses were in the barn. . . . Physical education had a horsemanship class. They came over, saddled and groomed the horses, and they'd ride the horses [in the barn]. . . . We lived down there a year—Jean and I did. We moved to the dairy barn, and our [fifteen-dollar] rent went up three dollars to eighteen dollars. I never will forget there was a rat in the dairy barn that was so big he'd challenge you. He wouldn't run off. He looked like a big tomcat. He'd stand flat-footed and get over there in your waste can. He was a dude. He was so big that you didn't want to [disturb him]. We knew where he came in the house. I got brave one night, and I plugged the thing [the hole] up where I could kill him. Hell, he challenged me. I unplugged the hole, let him out, and plugged it back up. That sucker was a dandy. **❞**

England persevered and continued to enjoy winning seasons and even bigger individual victories. One of his biggest moments occurred when his Indians beat Arkansas Tech, "the wonderboys" among Arkansas colleges of that day. In his words, "We never put up with second-rate citizenship in the State of Arkansas from that day on." England believed that a large part of winning athletic contests consisted of "the mental game." He explained how he prepared his athletes for the game against Tech:

❝ We started concentrating on that game on Monday. The game was to be played on Saturday night. Every day we sat in the stands, and nobody said anything—just everybody biting

old gymnasium next to the athletic field, I can see them yet—the boys sprawled around there in a circle before we went on the field. And I looked at them. And they were doing what they'd been doing for five to ten minutes before practice all week: biting their lips, kind of quivering, and concentrating. And I thought, 'Boy, I better shut up. I better not spoil this.' I didn't say a word. My lips started quivering. I saw tears fall. I said, 'Let's go.' Did they play ball! Oh my God, how

lower lip when I came over . . . in August. He [England] let us have the first two weeks of December [1953] off because the bowl game in Orlando, Florida, was played after Christmas. . . . That fever blister healed up in those weeks. September, October, November—I had a fever blister for four months. It'd dry up. I might go four or five days, and then someone would hit me in the mouth with a forearm or something, [and] it'd bleed. ❞

Barnhart and Lewis Halls, the first dormitories at the old "Aggie School," were razed to make way for the Carl R. Reng Center. Completed in 1964, the center provided a new focal point for student activities. The Wigwam was relocated in the center, along with a cafeteria, barber shop, billiard room, bowling alley, television and game rooms, bookstore, lounges, and other facilities.

his gums and sitting there thinking. I said, 'Concentrate. Concentrate. The greatest goal in football this team's ever had is going to be in your hands for about two hours Saturday night. Think! Think what it means for us to be more or less kicked around and thought of as second-rate and never have a chance to become first-rate. The chance comes two hours Saturday night.' . . . Usually I had studied what I would say ten minutes before a game. I had it all planned—what I was going to say. And in the

they played! Arkansas Tech wished they'd never heard of us. ❞

Bill Davidson endured England's excruciating practice sessions in his freshman year and never forgot them. Preparations for the Tangerine Bowl were so rigorous that he thought the "two-a-day" practices would never end:

❝ It was the longest thing. No face masks [were used then] . . . . I had a fever blister on my

England's players seldom complained about such Spartan circumstances on the practice field, since his punishments were even more severe. As Davidson recalled, many of the football players were young men from the streets of the northern cities. The head coach "knew how to handle the street kid" through strict discipline. Davidson remembered one form of punishment:

❝ If you had a bad practice, in his mind he'd think that you were loafing. You didn't eat. He just called Mrs. Nedrow who had the cafeteria then and said, '[This student] don't eat tonight.' A lot of those guys built up a real resentment towards Frosty. . . . He was a very hard-nosed guy. **"**

England closed out his career with the Indians on New Year's Day 1954 in a match-up with East Texas State College in the Tangerine Bowl. It was a triumph and a defeat. The game ended 6 to 6. England considered the tie to be a defeat. This score resulted from a freak event, when defensive back Danny Spensieri intercepted a pass and broke into the open field. He had a touchdown cinched when, suddenly, the unexpected happened. The former coach recalled that heartbreaking incident:

" I looked back to see who might have a chance of tackling him, and no one was close enough that I figured could get him. So I took my eyes off of Danny. As he ran by the East Texas State bench, when I next looked up the ball was on the ground bounding around. No one had tackled Danny. No one was within ten yards of him. And there was the ball on the ground. Pumping his arms, trying to get to that goal, the ball slipped out. The poor boy cried, and I think the coach almost shed a tear, too. And the game ended six to six. And East Texas State was still undefeated, and so were we. **"**

Although the A-State athletic program declined for a short time after the departure of Frosty England, the football team soon recovered under a new head coach, Gene Harlow. A Vanderbilt graduate, Harlow studied the techniques of Paul "Bear" Bryant. Bill Davidson observed that Harlow was "aggressive on the field," and he employed an assistant, King Block, who was equally forceful. Harlow desired that his players maintain an unusual degree of alertness off the practice field as well as on the gridiron. Davidson remembered that he often deliberately avoided the strongwilled man:

" I wouldn't even meet him on the sidewalk. He may grab you and get on you, or he may hit you with a forearm and knock you down. You

know that was his favorite thing. You never relaxed around him. Same way with the practice. You know your mind lingers off or something. He'd just see you, and first thing you know you'd be sitting on your tail because he'd come up and hit you with a forearm to get your attention. If he moved toward you, you moved away from him. You just kind of worked in a circle around him. **"**

In spite of this ferocious nature, Davidson concluded that "Everybody loved him . . . [and] respected him." Davidson adopted much of Harlow's coaching technique when he became head coach of the Indians in the 1970s.

One of the most important events in the growth of varsity sports on the A-State campus was the creation of a separate athletic department in 1959. In the past, physical education and athletics comprised a joint department. Coaches taught P.E. classes. While this separation of the two areas took place quietly, it symbolically paved the way for an even greater emphasis on organized sports at A-State. At the same time, this decision freed the physical education specialists for independent growth. Gladys Hudgins, a member of this staff since 1953, explained that she and her colleagues desired this separation from athletics because "physical education and athletics may be akin to each other, but they are certainly far apart, too":

" In physical education we're interested in education for all, for each individual. And in athletics you're really serving only the gifted population. . . . In physical education you're trying real hard to give them a broad base of activity and let them choose what they do better. And in athletics you are limited to a certain sport, and that may be the only one that you'd be involved with. **"**

Athletic director Tomlinson agreed with this assessment and believed that the physical education area deserved the leadership of a trained specialist with a doctorate in physical education:

" I got with Dr. Reng and said, 'There's some things in physical education that you need to get a man with his doctorate to head it up,' because I had gone as far as my training would let me go. I could do administration and that kind of stuff, but we got to the place where we needed some research done. We needed to have access to some things that I didn't have access to. . . . So he said, 'Let's find us a good, qualified man with his doctorate and make him director of physical education and let him develop . . . this department now to where it ought to be.' We went out and got Dr. [Linus J.] Dowell. He did an excellent job. **"**

With the creation of the separate athletic department, the sports program took on new vigor. In 1962 A-State joined the new Southland Conference. This event ended a long period of travail. Just as Arkansas State had surpassed its three agricultural high school counterparts after World War II—but failed to grow equal to the University of Arkansas—the institution had not fit into the Arkansas Intercollegiate Conference (AIC) or qualified for a major conference. Tomlinson recounted the history of this nettlesome problem and the eventual decision to abandon the smaller league:

" In '45, they called a meeting of the state colleges and revived the Arkansas Intercollegiate Conference that had been discontinued during the war. That was all the state's colleges, other than the university, plus Ouachita. At that time, Harding did not belong. So we stayed in that until 1951. We simply never could get a championship schedule, particularly in football. They would always use the excuse that we were so far away from the rest of them they couldn't travel up here. But it was always necessary that we travel to Monticello or Conway or Russellville. I kept telling the president we couldn't get enough games. . . . Finally, he decided Mr. [Dean B.] Ellis, the faculty [athletic] representative, and I were not men enough to get the job done. He went to Little Rock himself, and a couple of their presidents let him know very quickly he didn't mean any more than we did. **"**

Large-scale construction was a common sight in the late fifties and sixties as ASC prepared the physical plant for university status. Dormitory construction was an essential phase in accommodating the growing student population.

This negative reception finally convinced Reng that Tomlinson's story was true. He informed the athletic director that he had withdrawn A-State from the Arkansas Intercollegiate Conference:

" We became freelance, which is a very difficult thing, and stayed that way until the organization of the Southland Conference in '62. We tried to get in the Ohio Valley Conference with the Kentucky and Tennessee teams, but they didn't want to cross the [Mississippi] river. We had an opportunity to get into the Gulf States Conference at that time, which was Mississippi Southern, the four larger Louisiana schools, Chattanooga, maybe East Texas. We couldn't afford the travel. That went by the board. We didn't have the facilities or the money to get into the Missouri Valley Conference. Finally . . . we became part of the Southland Conference. **"**

The creation of Jumping Joe as a symbol for the Indians was another significant event connected with the athletic program. Arkansas State College had adopted the sobriquet, "Indians," in the 1930s but lacked a visual image to accompany the name. Tex Plunkett explained that some uncertainties accompanied the origins of this caricature of Native Americans:

" I always thought that a student by the name of Avery Knight developed that, but Dean Moore and Mr. Cameron are [at] loggerheads about that. Dean Moore says one thing, and Mr. Cameron says another. Mr. Cameron says he was designed for a milk carton, and Dean Moore said somebody else did it. I think that Avery Knight brought it into prominence. Along with the nickname, Indian, when race became such a conflicting thing, we were wondering. Stanford University changed their name, and we were wondering if we would have to change ours. Dr. Reng got ahold of the old chief of the tribe that used to be here and brought him down here, and the chief said, 'I like that.' **"**

The athletic program of A-State reached many persons in the college service area that otherwise might have remained untouched by this institution of higher education. As a publicity agency for the school, it had few peers. Phil Bridger, who attended the college and later coached in the public schools, recalled that the Northeast Arkansas Invitational Basketball Tournament, hosted by this campus, became a strong attraction for the Indians. Representatives of dozens of schools and hundreds of players, visited the college grounds for this event:

" I would say back then coming to the NEA Tournament was like going to the state tournament. It was 'the thing.' I remember that I was fortunate enough to play on a team that won it and coach a team that won it, and I felt when I played and when I was coaching, too, that probably the only thing that rivaled the NEA Tournament was the state tournament in your mind and the kids' minds, too. Back then you had a lot more schools, smaller schools, but more of them, and to get a bid to the NEA

Tournament was hard to do, and you really cherished it. **"**

The most conspicuous evidence of the growth of Arkansas State in the 1950s and 1960s was the remarkable expansion of the physical plant. When Carl R. Reng assumed the presidency in 1951, inadequacies of the buildings were most glaring. He recalled the sight that awaited him in that year:

" The buildings' maintenance was terrible. Our appropriation that first year was $250,000. That wouldn't go very far today, but in those days we really didn't have a lot. So I knew that some of the things that we had to do in order to cause the college to move forward was have the facilities to do it. I know that the education part of the program is important, but you got to have the facilities to back up the education, and we just didn't have it. So I immediately started out to try to get some facilities for the students—for the faculty to have. **"**

The new executive set out to overcome this formidable handicap to the growth of ASC. Within a few years, the campus bristled with many new structures. Taken together, they constituted a collection fit for a university.

The campus also expanded laterally, as many acres of land were annexed adjacent to the college grounds and elsewhere. President Reng took the initiative in the acquisition of property and the construction of buildings. Shortly after he arrived in Jonesboro in 1951, the college purchased a president's home near the campus. The National Guard Armory, which also housed the ROTC department, was begun in 1955. Two dormitories, additional faculty housing, and a new and larger trailer village were added. New classroom space became available when the demonstration school was discontinued in the education building.

A remarkable enlargement of the educational complex took place in 1955 when the college annexed Beebe Junior College. This school had fallen onto economic hard times, local citizens were abusing its vacant buildings, and the legislature threatened to close the facility. Other four-year institutions refused to annex the Beebe educational facility even though they were nearer to that community. "But anyway," recalled Reng, "they came up here and asked us if we'd take them. So I went to great detail to check them out" and confirmed that the junior college was in bad condition. However, the president concluded that annexation could have a long-range benefit for Arkansas State, since that region elected several senators and representatives to the state legislature. Naturally, they would assist A-State. Reng explained other helpful consequences of the merger:

  ❝ At that time Orville Cheney, who had been president of the board of trustees when I was hired, was then working in the state treasurer's department. I went down to talk to Orville. He . . . talked about Beebe—he said, 'It's a mess.' I said, 'I know it.' [He] says, 'I'm going to tell you something that nobody probably has remembered, that Senator [W.H.] Abington who was the man who had really gotten Beebe Junior College as a political gift at one time back there had passed a wine tax and nobody has ever made an appropriation from that wine tax fund.' And he said, 'Do you know there's about $90,000 in the state treasury that has accumulated from that old wine tax?' Well, knowing that was all I needed to know. I figured I could build the junior college up enough to make the people happy because $90,000 went quite a ways in those days. And so I said, 'Oh boy, that's just what I need.' So we went back, and we had a bill drawn in which they turned Beebe Junior College over to Arkansas State and the next thing, we introduced a bill to appropriate the $90,000 and had a bunch of legislators whose jaws dropped pretty low that we got it passed. ❞

    This effort to construct a physical plant fit for a university received a considerable boost from Governor Orville Faubus. This energetic and facile politician took a keen interest in educational funding as Eugene Smith, longtime official of Arkansas State and now president, explained:

  ❝ He did not find himself able to go to college and participate in higher education. . . . He was

ASC suffered serious damage from a tornado in 1961. The roof of the drill hall (fieldhouse) was torn off, along with the roof of the old physical education building. Kell Field, then south of the hangar, also was destroyed and was later moved to its present location.

A cultural advantage offered by A-State was the study-tour abroad. Mildred Vance (second from left) escorted this 1961 group that visited Michelangelo Square in Florence, Italy as part of a nine-country tour.

very impressed with what higher education could do for the state, the people, and young people. I found he was very much in favor of programs supporting higher education. He had supported this program and the passage of the package of taxes that retired the bond. On a general obligation bond issue in Arkansas—as you know the people have to vote to issue those bonds—the people turned that down. So he then devised a system where those taxes would flow into what was named the State Institutional Buildings Construction Fund, and the state had the enormous so-called surplus then of $8 million. So he called a special session and convinced the legislature to appropriate that $8 million. This [Dean B. Ellis] Library building was the first building on this campus funded by the State of Arkansas. **"**

Under the auspices of the new fund, the campus blossomed with substantial buildings. Renovation had already begun in April 1961 after a fierce wind struck the grounds. Several structures were improved, including a fieldhouse for basketball and a considerably improved gymnasium. A new post office was completed after Reng made several trips to Washington to obtain permission to build a federal building on state property. He reflected:

" I'll have to give Mr. [E.C.] 'Took' Gathings, who was our state representative up in Washington at that time, a lot of credit. Mr. Gathings went over to the Post Office Department and beat the table and everything else and they finally agreed we could provide the money and build it on state property. In other

words, we changed the national regulation so we could build it, and we got the money, and we did build the post office. **"**

The list of structures erected in the 1960s was formidable. Among them were the Dean B. Ellis Library; two women's dormitories, Arkansas Hall and Kays Hall; the new administration building; Seminole Twin Towers, a men's residence hall; the fine arts building; the laboratory sciences building; and a radio-journalism building. Several facilities, including the old science building and Wilson Hall, were substantially renovated.

Certainly the most ambitious of these new edifices was the student union, named the Carl R. Reng Center. The projected expenditure soon increased many times over. Reng, the proponent of this project, recounted some of the history of this ambitious undertaking:

" I first told the board of trustees I thought we could build one for $500,000. They said, 'Well, that would be fine.' They thought we had ought to have something like that. So I started touring the country. I was going up to Southern Illinois and up to Champaign, Illinois, and some of these other big colleges. Looked at their student unions. Every time I looked I began to see my figure would have to go up. . . . I went back to the board the third time, I believe. I told them it would be around $2.5 million. Well, that's quite a difference between $500,000 that I talked about originally. But I had worked it out. Mr. Cameron was . . . really good on finances, and he had it worked out where we thought that we could build that building and borrow the money, and the income from the building itself would amortize it. Which it has done over the years . . . so it has been a $2.5 million gift to the State of Arkansas. If you had to build it today, it would cost you at least five million, and so it has been a real asset to the university to have. As you notice, it was not called the student center, and there was method in our madness on that. We could not get a loan for student centers at that time. They just weren't making loans. But they would make a loan on a more commercial thing. So we called it really a civic center that we were going to serve banquets for the people uptown and Chamber of Commerce, and we were able to get the money on that basis. **"**

Linual Cameron emphasized the unique nature of this building:

" I worked five years on getting the money and what a student center should be. . . . One school had built one that to me was only a glorified lounge. It was not a student center, and I wanted a student center for the school. I visited no telling how many student centers, and the student center of twenty-five or thirty years ago was not a center. It was a gymnasium. That is what it amounted to. **"**

Eventually, Reng persuaded the federal government to contribute to the project. Here again, Arkansas' delegation in the national capitol contributed immeasurably to the success of the student center. When the time came for a decisive turn of events in Washington, Cameron recalled that he approached Reng: "Dr. Reng, do you want to do it [make the journey] or do you want me to do it?" The president replied, "'I will,' and he called [Senator] Bill Fulbright and we had [it] approved." Soon a federal official arrived to examine the plans. With that the Reng Center became a reality.

This monumental building campaign transformed a modest college physical plant into a modern, serviceable aggregation of educational buildings that could accommodate a mature academic community. The buildings seemed to encapsulate all of the developments at A-State that had occurred since Carl Reng took office in 1951. From a small, remote campus with relatively few structures and a limited curriculum, the institution had mushroomed into an impressive collection of buildings with varied course offerings. Many forces contributed to this rapid expansion. The prosperity of the post-war era promoted a slow and possibly not-so-obvious change in the attitudes of citizens toward higher education. By the mid-1960s, many inhabitants of eastern Arkansas regarded a college degree as essential to the futures of their children. The career orientation of big businesses exerted a steady pressure upon young people to obtain the diploma. As the small family farm yielded to corporate farming, sons and daughters of the old yeomanry sought out Arkansas State College as a place to prepare for a meaningful career. The energies of President Reng, his staff, and the college faculty allowed the school to capitalize on the opportunities offered by the new social conditions. By the 1960s the former agricultural high school had outgrown even its state college identity. A-State was ready to forge a new identity for itself: that of Arkansas State University.

This 1962 aerial view of the campus looks west from the present location of Stadium Boulevard.

CHAPTER VI

"TO MOST OF US IT WAS THE CROWNING ACHIEVEMENT"

A Time for Definition

When A-State attained university status in 1967, this event marked not only the culmination of a decade of effort, but the beginning of a new stage in the school's development. Once the legislature had conferred university status, the newly elevated school had to demonstrate an ability not only to function as a university but to carry out the responsibilities that accompanied the new title. Thus the institution devoted the late 1960s and early 1970s to the search for an identity as a university in more than name only. But acquiring that name was the necessary first step in the definition process.

Preparations for acquisition of university status required many years of work by the entire college community as well as the dedicated support of citizens and public officials in northeast Arkansas. The work of the faculty and staff immediately after World War II contributed to this quest. Their success in responding to the various educational needs of a growing student body assumed a "building block" effect, according to Ike Tomlinson who joined the faculty in 1943. When Arkansas State College achieved success in one endeavor, such as the accommodation of the veterans, this victory made possible subsequent successes. The cumulative effect eventually led to university status:

❝ I think the decade of 1960 to '70 was tremendously influenced by the growth of the community and the student body and the faculty in the late fifties, and it seemed to me that it was stimulated by the success that was evident

with the handling of the [student] GIs. This began to create opportunities for more planning—well, maybe I better say more ambitious planning. The university status became a common topic of conversation [in the 1950s], the various accreditation groups were brought to the campus, and a number of departments and the university itself achieved accreditation in various areas that ten years before . . . had seemed out of reach. That gave added stimulus to the attention the public paid [to ASC] and the ambitions of the faculty and the students, and then an effort was made to attain university status [in 1959], and that failed. Quite possibly it should have the first time, and I think we all agreed on that later. But it sowed the seed for the planning for the final push to receive university status, and . . . no doubt to most of us it was the crowning achievement. ❞

When the administration asked the legislature for this much-desired elevation in 1959, President Reng and his associates anxiously sought every means to influence senators and representatives. Robert Ferralasco, member of the business faculty, remembered one publicity measure that upset some of the faculty:

❝ It was suggested very strongly that each faculty member chip in—I think it was ten dollars—to buy each legislator a cowboy hat, Stetson hats. I think most of us chipped in. A few didn't. I'm not quite sure whether the AAUP met over that, but the Faculty Association [did]. . . . We were a little bit concerned. . . . Of course, ten dollars in those days was quite a large chunk out of our salary. ❞

The initial bid for university status and a second attempt in the next session failed to pass the legislature. Reng could not forget the humiliation, though he detected some fear among the opposition that even in defeat ASC had made some gains:

❝ All the other colleges and the University [of Arkansas] and everybody was against us. [But] they had a feeling our enrollment was growing, and we were moving right ahead. Of course, [in] the next session of the legislature we made another run for the university status, but we knew the only reason we made the run then—we made it half-heartedly—we just wanted to keep it [the issue] alive. 🙰

Most of the opposition to A-State's ambitions lay in the region around the University of Arkansas at Fayetteville and, to a lesser degree, around the state capital. William Wyatt, who served on the board of trustees during these important years, discussed the composition of the opposition:

🙰 The *Arkansas Gazette's* editor just didn't think we ought to have another university at that time. He fought it *every* way he could. Governors were really not too committed to it. They would've signed the bill, but as far as getting out and actually working for it, they wouldn't do it, so you had to work through the legislature to get it done. 🙰

Advocates of university status for Arkansas State College were especially dismayed when they failed to receive the complete support of the northeast Arkansas community. That is not to say that people in the immediate vicinity of the institution did not want the college to grow. In fact, senators and representatives from northeast Arkansas devoted long and tireless hours on behalf of university status. But among some people hesitancy existed. Ike Tomlinson shrewdly attributed this surprising attitude to the fierce loyalty of many northeast Arkansans to the Razorbacks:

🙰 It was not pleasant to say anything about university status among most of the people. . . . Frankly, they had one university [at Fayetteville], and that was enough. 🙰

This devotion to the distant campus had developed for almost a century. "Suddenly a group of out-of-state people" under Carl Reng at ASC "came in and told them how to run" higher education, added Tomlinson. Perhaps this attitude should not have surprised the A-State community, since residents of this area in the 1910s had held the same notions about V.C.

An aerial photograph taken in 1969 shows the Arkansas State University campus looking west from Aggie Road.

Kays, an Illinoian, and the instructors that he employed from outside Arkansas.

With each failure to obtain university status, Reng and his followers redoubled their efforts, both on campus and at large. One of the most common arguments against the qualifications of the college for this recognition was the absence of a university-class library. The current facility existed in the basement of Wilson Hall and contained a collection hardly adequate even for a college. Reng recalled the efforts of his administration to overcome this handicap:

66 Oh boy, we were in real trouble. We were put on probation . . . with the [North Central Association] accrediting agency until we got the [Dean B.] Ellis Library. When we constructed the Ellis Library, we cut it back so we had $100,000. We bought books [with those funds]. From that time on we began to improve our status. 99

William Wyatt explained how officials of the college continued to cultivate the support of important politicians:

66 Dr. Reng worked with the leadership in the House. . . . He convinced . . . [them] that we had to have it done. . . . We had real good help in the Senate. The senator from Hot Springs was the one that cast the deciding vote to get it going back then. He could've had anything he wanted at Arkansas State that night. He did a good job. Gene Fleeman from over here [eastern Arkansas] was the president of the House of Representatives. . . . He did everything he could to work on it. He gave us lists of people on certain committees. I've gone by and picked them up and taken them over to board meetings where we could check with them. 99

Wyatt and the other board members worked tirelessly—and without pay—for university status. He recalled that they "made seventeen trips to Little Rock during the year," 1966, that led to the final victory in the legislature.

On that critical day, January 17, 1967, when Arkansas State College's biggest bid for this coveted promotion was slated, an enthusiastic crowd of academic officials, politicians, and well-

wishers descended upon the capitol building. Reng described these final preparations and the frenzied atmosphere that prevailed in the legislative halls:

66 About three weeks, I'd say, before the session started, Woodrow Haynes [farm superintendent], Dr. Gene Smith, myself, and Linual Cameron went to Little Rock. Gene Smith and Woodrow Haynes were together, and Cameron was helping me. I was sitting in a hotel room on the telephone, and Gene Smith and Woodrow Haynes were in the car. I was calling senators [and] representatives . . . in all parts of the state, making appointments for them [Smith and Haynes]. 99

As Reng explained, Smith and Haynes drove to all parts of the state to visit legislators to get their signatures for the bill. He continued:

66 So when it came time for the bill to come up, we had a great many more than enough [votes] for the House. We had it cinched. They had already agreed they were going to pass it, but we were six votes short in the Senate. . . . So we got our friends to turn the heat on. Of course, as you know, it passed 85 to 17 in the House, and it passed the Senate pretty well. But we were worried. 99

That long-awaited moment occurred in the Senate when Senator Clifton Wade, a leading opponent, conceded defeat. Reng recalled:

66 I never shall forget. . . . Senator Wade always represented the University of Arkansas in Fayetteville. That was his prime job as senator, and 'Deacon' Wade, of course, had to be against this bill. But that day we had all the figures [on our side], and he knew it. He got up and took the floor of the Senate. He said, 'Now, gentlemen, I'm against the bill. I have to be. But I hear the bells ringing and the whistle blowing, and I'm getting off the damn track.' 99

As the participants in this drive for recognition of higher education in northeast Arkansas reflected upon this important event, they marveled at the great strides made by

Even though the 1959 bid for university status was successful, more than 3,000 students welcomed Carl Reng back to the campus.

Arkansas State since Carl R. Reng assumed the presidency in 1951. At the same time, most recognized that the real work was only beginning. Since 1967 the institution has toiled to establish an identity as a university in size and physical facilities, program development, and increased opportunities for students and faculty.

Surface events of the late 1960s and early 1970s were not particularly auspicious for the fledgling university. At times the institution experienced dislocating forces similar to the distractions that had promoted instability in the 1940s. A comparison of the eras reveals some important similarities as well as vital differences. For instance, in the early 1940s and in the years around 1970, the school faced the problems engendered by war. While the Vietnam conflict of the latter period did not drain students from the campus as World War II had done, the fighting in Southeast Asia divided the campus and revealed to administrators that an aroused, sometimes strident and vocal student body and faculty had to be reckoned with. Moreover, in both eras long-term presidents vacated their positions and were followed by several short-term executives.

Clearly times were difficult for persons seeking to satisfy both the need for stability and the rights of students and faculty to freedom of expression. Robert Moore, then dean of students at ASU, characterized the era succinctly: "There was a period in the late sixties and early seventies that was probably the most traumatic of any period on anybody's campus." Speaking from the student perspective, Dannye Pierce, who was president of the ASU Student Government Association during the most intense period of student unrest, mused:

66 I think that we students . . . were forced to grow up. I really faced some tough social questions, and we had to make decisions about what our positions on these difficulties were going to be. **99**

The catalyst for unrest was the country's involvement in military action in Vietnam. History professor John Galloway observed the initial effects of that conflict among personnel at ASU:

E.L. Angell, director of the Commission on Coordination of Higher Education Finance, enumerated reasons for withholding university status. Although opposition to university status continued, success was achieved in 1967.

Carl Reng (front row, fifth from left) waited with ASU supporters in the legislative gallery for university status vote.

" I think there was not a lot of concern. There were those, yes, who felt that we should not be there [in Vietnam], and there was some who were farsighted enough to fear that we were going to get much too involved, but still there were many who were inclined to support this action [United States involvement] out of their concern over seeing another nation overrun by communism. And I guess most of us did not have the foresight to see what would develop. **"**

As the fear that American intervention in Vietnam might not be in either country's best interests grew on the ASU campus, students and faculty began to demonstrate publicly against the war. Such outspoken action was unprecedented on the Jonesboro campus. Galloway described one demonstration:

" A memorial service was held in the auditorium here in which a number of short talks were made by faculty members, and several persons . . . both faculty and students—read the names and addresses of quite a long list of Arkansas soldiers or servicemen who had been killed in Vietnam. Now this was not any wild demonstration. It was a very solemn memorial service, I think, done in good taste. **"**

Yet everyone did not share Galloway's assessment of the nature of the demonstration. He continued:

" It seemed to have aroused some antagonism from some quarters on the campus, both in the administration and among some faculty members, who felt that it was somehow . . . disloyal . . . to take this means of criticizing our involvement in Vietnam. **"**

Some other demonstrations against the conflict, though, were more strident. Dannye Pierce remembered "a little jeering" at a strategically placed demonstration outside the president's office window.

Other sources of protest existed on the ASU campus and provoked additional tension. "The black students were beginning to come on in rather large numbers," recalled Robert Moore, "and they were protesting [the song] 'Dixie.'" Blacks also conducted sit-ins out of sympathy for oppressed members of their race elsewhere. Other matters aroused both black and white students, including the mandatory ROTC program and the dismissal of some faculty members for what students thought to be insufficient causes. Pierce chaired a meeting of the SGA when the issue of mandatory vs. voluntary ROTC resulted in some hastily spoken words:

❝ We thought we had Dean Moore's commitment to support voluntary ROTC, and then in our opinion he backed out of that commitment. And I recall . . . just verbally blistering [him]. I was so mad I couldn't see straight. And I called the meeting, read my statement, and adjourned the meeting. ❞

A subsequent personal interview with the dean convinced the SGA president that he had reacted without fully understanding Moore's position. In fact, Pierce attributed the lack of more serious student unrest on the ASU campus during this turbulent period to Moore's good judgment.

Although some sporadic violence occurred, student protestors lacked concentrated direction, according to Eugene Smith, dean of the graduate school at the time:

❝ There [were] some fires on campus. There were thirty-eight [caliber] bullets [fired] through the front of the administration building [and] bricks through the glass walls of the president's office. ❞

Yet he added quickly, "I do not personally know anyone that can say who did these things. Whether they were off-campus or on-campus people is unclear."

Robert Moore recalled one incident when level heads in the administration prevented a potentially explosive situation from becoming really serious:

Governor Winthrop Rockefeller, who signed the legislation that created ASU, was one of several state and national celebrities to visit A-State during the 1960s. Increasingly, the campus attracted well-known figures from various fields of endeavor.

❝ This particular night somebody had set fire to the old abandoned fine arts-engineering building. It was empty. It was going to be torn down. A firetruck came into the campus, and a couple of patrol cars came with it. The students heard it in big Twin Towers [residence hall]. . . . They all came out to see what was going on. They put it out in about nothing flat, but all the local police authorities hit the panic button, and before it was all over, there were probably seventy-five policemen out there. I counted seventeen state police cars. All the auxiliary policemen here in town were out there. All the sheriff's office and deputies [were] out there. They didn't know what to do. The students were having a big time. They were yelling at them—I guess calling them a few choice names, as students will do. And they [the police] wanted to start something—make those students get back in the buildings, and I told them they couldn't do it—that what they [the officers] ought to do is leave. Well, they didn't see that. Here was three or four hundred students out there, maybe more than that, and they [police] thought they had to do something. Well, I finally made them mad and convinced them they ought to leave and get away right now, and we'd put the students to bed. And so they moved out. We did—we put the students to bed. ❞

The dean of students tended to minimize the importance of the various protests. "There were only about one or two percent of the students even involved in any of the movements," he said. However, the administration made plans to react to violent demonstrations. Eugene Smith recalled that the governor required ASU "to devise and put in print a campus reaction plan." He explained the thinking behind such a plan:

❝ One was led to believe at that time that there were people interested in disrupting the university and that those people were quite capable, quite intelligent, and quite well organized. And they knew about as much about this university and its power sources and its communication lines . . . as we knew ourselves. ❞

137

Celebrations followed the signing of the university status bill on January 17, 1967. Tex Plunkett reads the first copy of The Herald *announcing university passage, while students talk to a radio reporter outside Wilson Hall and celebrate in ASU's Wigwam.*

When asked if the administration believed the threat of student unrest was serious, Smith replied that, given the campus unrest across the nation:

66 It was considered to be deadly serious by all that were involved. The prevailing attitude as I recall it was . . . that this is a nation . . . of law. And law would be preserved. And that if you want things changed, you don't do it by burning down the university. The law says you can't burn it down, and therefore the state, acting through the governor's office and down through the institutions [of higher education], will take those steps necessary to preserve the law and order on campuses. 99

One surprisingly positive outcome of student protest was the drafting of a student rights document. Robert Moore attended a summer program at Michigan State University that provided administrators with constructive strategies for responding to student activism. From information gathered there Moore "put together a student rights and freedoms document that set forth what this university really believed in and espoused the right of students for freedom of speech, freedom of assembly, and due process." Consequently, out of turmoil that might have weakened a less mature institution, ASU more clearly defined its position on academic freedom, at least as the concept applied to the student body.

Like their counterparts on campuses across the United States, some ASU faculty members began to speak out against abuses of administrative power. They advocated goals for the university that differed from those of the president and his associates. In most cases, the conflicts were minor. Such was not the case in the spring of 1970 when a clash occurred between the history department and the administration. John Galloway, chairman of the department at that time, described the situation:

66 As the time for issuing contracts neared, I was told that it was very questionable as to whether some of the members of the department would be offered contracts for the following year.

In fact, more than that—I was told that several individuals would not be, and I became upset over this and began to try to find the reasons for it. I still don't . . . know the reasons. There [were] some reasons given which I did not regard as sufficiently valid. 99

Galloway cited a problematic case:

66 One concerned the question of rehiring one of the women in the department . . . because she

Sorority rush is a big moment for those desiring to join a social organization. Fraternities and sororities continued to flourish during the 1970s at ASU and engaged in a variety of philanthropic as well as social activities.

had discovered after the semester started that she was pregnant and delivered a baby just at the end of the fall semester. And there was extreme reluctance to renew her contract because there was some feeling on the part somewhere in the administration that she had caused considerable difficulty and imposed a hardship on administrators and upon other members of the department by her absence. 99

The woman had been able to complete all of her duties for the fall, the only problem being that

the birth had resulted in her getting her final grades computed a few hours after the deadline. Such insensitive personnel decisions posed a serious threat to the integrity of the university, Galloway believed.

Another contributing factor to the potential for turmoil on the ASU campus was the changing moral code of the student body. According to housing director Phil Bridger, modern students began to demonstrate "lack of discretion" about sensitive personal subjects that their parents

would not have discussed in public. He elaborated:

66 Young ladies are much more free with [personal] information now than they used to be. You know, I think that it took much more of an adjustment for me than it did for them. I had been raised in a society where they didn't say those things. They are just liable to come in and say now that ' She's a lesbian, I don't want to live with her; [or] I'm tired, I can't sleep at night, her boyfriend is sleeping with her in the next bed, ' or

even worse. They really don't put any fancy names on it. They just tell it like it is. 🟊🟊

Yet not everything the students did during the late 1960s and early 1970s smacked of the high-minded seriousness that characterized protest activities. Dannye Pierce, a member of Sigma Pi fraternity at ASU, described an incident that could have occurred virtually anytime on an American college campus:

🟊🟊 We went up to Sand Creek—our fraternity did—and had a stag party one night and got involved in an altercation with some of the local people. The next night the Tekes [Tau Kappa Epsilon] and . . . Lambda Chi [Alpha] took their dates up there. And they were going to have a weenie roast or something like that. The locals couldn't distinguish between [fraternities] . . . so the locals began an altercation with that group that brought the Greene County Sheriff's department out there. And the Lambda Chis and Tekes got caught and were put on social probation, and they never knew about us. 🟊🟊

Robert Moore also recalled a relatively lighthearted manifestation of student rebellion against traditional mores—streaking:

🟊🟊 Just the week before spring break—that would have been about 1974—it hit. And it was a beautiful week. The nights were warm. I saw three to four thousand people lining the streets out on Dean Street. They weren't all students either—townspeople [were there]. There was some streaking. It was dark and not much exposure, but there were a lot of people got uptight about it—thought somebody ought to do something and really wasn't much you could do, but let it run its course. And I fought the battle to let it run its course, and I had total student support for that attitude. When they left for spring holidays, I made the statement that it would probably be over. And it was. And we came back, and it was all forgotten, and there was no more of it. 🟊🟊

In dealing with the new liberated lifestyle of its students, ASU responded with considerable

Lines of communication were maintained during tense moments by Robert Moore, dean of students.

flexibility. For the most part, unless the behavior of a student was clearly disruptive to the functioning of the university, that behavior was ignored.

Despite student and faculty unrest, the institution continued to grow. Major additions to the physical plant occurred during the years following the attainment of university status. The old National Guard Armory, built in 1927 and later used as a physical education building, gave way to a modern physical education and health sciences complex. Agricultural and laboratory sciences facilities, along with a new fine arts center, were completed. With a generous grant from the university's long-term benefactors, the Wilson family, a student health center was erected behind the Reng Center.

Perhaps most striking to the public eye—and most controversial—was the construction of a new athletic complex, including a football stadium to replace the aging Kays Field and a modern track. Former President Reng related the maneuvering that was required to obtain the funding for the stadium project. The first step was planning:

❝ Well, I knew we needed a stadium. I didn't know how to go about getting it. It's the same old money problem we'd always had. So we decided we'd try to raise it with funds and gifts and so forth. We hired a group [of consultants] to come in, and I found out that all they did was draw you a blueprint. And you had to do all the work anyway. So we dismissed them. We just went to work. **❞**

Reng and his staff were very successful in their attempts to raise funds from private donors:

❝ We made calls, we pleaded, and we did this, and we did that. We finally raised a million, six hundred thousand dollars or whatever it was. So we built the stadium. . . . That's the hardest job I had to do out there. I hate to ask people for money, but I knew we had to do it. You know, it's lucky that we built it when we did. That thing would cost you what? Four million today? It was built just at the right time. It's a fine stadium, and it can be added on to. That stadium is so

ASU students responded to policy matters—both local and national—with campus demonstrations. United States involvement in Vietnam was a major protest issue.

constructed that new wings can be put on to seat 60,000 eventually. 🙄

The state rounded out the project with a supplemental appropriation for construction of the facility.

Having raised the money, the problems were just beginning. Reng's plans for locating the stadium on the northeastern edge of the campus conflicted with state highway department plans:

66 They built this new [State Highway 49] bypass through the campus. If you come across the bypass now on the viaduct, if you'll look and follow the section line which they always do, they go right through the middle of our stadium. We hadn't built the stadium yet, but I knew that's where I wanted to build it. So when they started laying that bypass out, I threw a fit. Because they had it staked out right down the section and wouldn't have left room on either side of the road to build a stadium. 🙄

The president's response to the proposed route for the bypass revealed that the university had attained enough power to flex its muscles in order to get what it wanted:

66 Well, they were going through college land, and I had a hard time getting them to swing that highway out and around. I threatened to charge

By the late sixties, the growing black student population had begun to register its demands for minority rights. In 1970, their concerns were quite visible through demonstrations and sit-ins.

them $10,000 an acre for every acre they used of college land if they didn't. And if they did [alter the route], we'd give it to them. Well, I was bluffing because I didn't think I could charge them for state land in the first place. . . . [But] we did convince the highway department. As you come across that viaduct [today] if you'll notice, it swings out and goes around the stadium. **"**

Other developments occurred that reflected the newly won status of "university." For example, the campus was soon divided into colleges: liberal arts, science, agriculture, fine arts, education, and business. (A temporary division into "schools" preceded this more permanent change.) By 1973, radio-television, journalism, and printing had been combined into a new College of Communications, and two independent divisions existed: nursing and ROTC. A University College provided students with individualized services in counseling, testing, tutoring, and general advisement for undecided majors. The place of the Graduate School became more firmly established in 1973 when the North Central Association of Colleges and Schools awarded the university mature status at the master's degree level. A further advanced degree in education, the specialist degree, had been added in 1969.

The development of the radio-television program illustrated the rapid advance of educational programs during the decade following university status. Charles Rasberry, chairman of this department, recalled that an important milestone occurred in 1967 when "we moved from Wilson Hall to what is now the computer center." Moreover, he added, "We increased our power from 760 watts to 3600 watts." A new radio tower also contributed to the growing program:

" We just had a short pole on top of Wilson [at first], but when we moved . . . we had to look around for a tower site. [There] was an old golf course out there [in the vicinity of the present Indian Stadium] then, and there was a hill as you came towards the old golf course. And our tower was located there. And then when we went to 100,000 watts [in 1973], of course, again to a

Serious demonstrations gave way in the mid-seventies to more light-hearted forms of expression. ASU students adopted the streaking craze.

143

certain extent we had to move because they were getting ready to build the stadium, and as a matter of fact they were working on roads going into the stadium before we got moved. We were knocked off the air a couple of times by backhoes digging out in that area, but we found a tall hill out in an area north of town. And the university purchased ten acres out there, and we built our transmitter building and put our [present] tower out there. 🙶

Although much of the radio and television equipment is costly and sophisticated, Rasberry emphasized that students participated in all aspects of broadcasting at KASU. This policy, contrary to common practice on many other campuses, remains a central feature of the ASU program.

In additon to academic service, the radio station performed valuable public service. Rasberry recalled how KASU began to disseminate information about weather alerts to northeast Arkansas during the frightful storms of the 1970s:

🙶 About three-thirty one Monday morning . . . we had . . . [a] storm, and I remember waking up and thinking it sounded like a bad storm to me. And I remember thinking, 'If I'm going to be blown away, I may as well be blown away at the station telling other people what's happening.' That sounds maybe kind of corny, but that really crossed my mind. So I remember jumping up and getting in the car and coming out to the station and signing the station on the air, calling the weather service. Got here in about ten minutes or so, signed on about three-forty, called the weather service. . . . They were just getting ready to issue this tornado warning. 'And it's for your county.' We put it on the air, and I began to talk about it—you know, what was happening—and stayed on the air until our regular morning man came in at six. 🙶

The response to this early-morning weather broadcast was enthusiastic, Rasberry recalled. "The telephone was ringing off the wall. . . . We got calls from everywhere. . . . I think it was up in the hundreds that day."

Courses in television were added to the curriculum shortly after the department moved out of Wilson Hall. A grant was instrumental in getting the program started. Both radio and television programs have enjoyed considerable success at ASU. The department chairman noted:

🙶 I'm very proud of the fact that our students—our graduates—have always been in demand. . . . It is a source of great pride to me to go, for example, to a meeting of the Arkansas Broadcasters Association and look around that room of station managers and operators and news directors and people and recognize that so many of those are our graduates. . . . We have them in major cities like Houston, Dallas, New York, Washington. . . . We have them all over. 🙶

Eugene Smith offered further testimony to this success:

🙶 Radio and television and journalism are fields where this institution has carved a position for itself. . . . Certainly if you traveled in the State of Arkansas, almost anywhere in the state, and ask what is the best place to study radio, television, [and] journalism, probably the answer . . . would be Arkansas State. And that probably extends into the Mid-South area. 🙶

In addition to enlarging the physical plant and augmenting the curriculum offerings, a third aspect of ASU's movement toward university identity was a broadening of opportunity for students and faculty. This situation was evident particularly in the increased minority involvement on campus. In the early days of Aggie the only black faces on campus were occasional members of the support staff such as Fannie Cash, a cook in Mother Warr's dining room. It was not until the mid-1950s that blacks were enrolled as students. Although the numbers of blacks increased during the next decade, some did not feel completely comfortable at the university. Calvin Smith, who later became the first black faculty member on campus, recalled his surprise at the cordial reception he received when he began graduate work at ASU in 1968. Smith had attended predominantly black schools and was employed in a similar educational environment in Helena,

Arkansas, when he began taking summer courses at the university. As he said:

🙶 Frankly, I was somewhat surprised at the reception. Most of them [ASU faculty members] were quite receptive. The first two professors I had here the very first summer [were] Dr. [Roger] Lambert and Dr. [Donald] Konold. . . . And I had no problems with them at all. They were quite helpful. 🙶

Yet the experience of other blacks was not as pleasant. Jane Gates, who became a political science professor and the first black woman instructor at ASU, remembered some of the problems that her fellow blacks experienced with some professors in the early 1970s:

🙶 The word got around, 'Don't take this guy. He's prejudiced.' You know, 'He's a racist. Don't take this class because it doesn't make any difference how well you do. You're still going to get [a] C, D, or an F. You know, you can't make any better than a C in the class.' 🙶

The black students focused much of their protest in the late 1960s upon one point of contention—the song "Dixie." The ASU Marching Band featured this old minstrel song regularly at football games. While whites may have been insensitive to some of the racial implications of this piece of music, the blacks associated it with plantations and slavery. Dannye Pierce, president of the Student Government Association in 1969-70, recalled the intensity of black student feelings in regard to this offensive tune and the procedure they used to place pressure upon the administration to abandon "Dixie":

🙶 I remember meetings . . . over the 'Dixie' thing. That's when Philander Smith College [in Little Rock] brought . . . two or three bus loads of their students up here and protested at the football game. I remember Carl Rowan [a nationally known black writer] . . . came here and spoke. 🙶

Pierce also attended meetings of the Jonesboro Council on Human Relations, which expressed a sincere interest in the condition of

Changing fashions in clothing and hairstyles joined psychedelic music as manifestations of the counter-culture that was sweeping college campuses in the late 1960s.

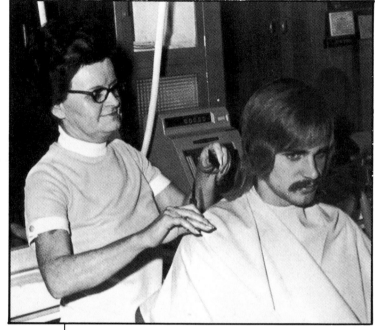

Student broadcaster Doug Rogers operated the control board of radio station KASU in its old studios in Wilson Hall.

Charles Rasberry, chairman of the radio-television department, welcomed the addition of television equipment to his department's facilities.

The addition of new and more sophisticated printing technology introduced ASU students to the latest developments in this field.

Academic opportunities were enhanced with the construction of modern library facilities. Dedication of the Dean B. Ellis Library in 1963 honored long-time mathematics professor Dean Ellis, whose generosity made the facility possible. Shown at the dedication ceremony are (from left) board of trustees members Russell Owen and Max Poe, Mrs. Ellis, Dean B. Ellis, Carl Reng, and Governor Orval Faubus.

black students at ASU.

Particularly aware of the tensions caused by "Dixie," Donald Minx related how he and the band decided to discard "Dixie":

❝ The first time I went to an event down here [in Arkansas] and they played 'Dixie' and everybody stood up, I didn't know what they stood up for. . . . I sat down because I didn't know what was coming off. Of course, that [song] was a big thing. The band plays 'Dixie'

and, wow, sets the world on fire. So we played 'Dixie' for quite a few years. . . . By my own choice, rather than being moved to it by necessity, I just one year closed the door to the band room and told the kids, 'I don't expect you to agree with me, but the [racial] problems are such that I think in the best interest of this organization and this institution, I am not going to put a piece of music in the folios this year that we have played for years. I don't want to make any big to-do about it. I will make no announcement about it. We just simply don't have it in the folios, and we will find another spirited tune to take the place of it.' So I lost a few friends over it and kept a few kids from getting beat up by doing it. ❞

Pierce noted how the ultimate decision not to use "Dixie" affected white students:

❝ That doesn't sound like much today, but emotions were real high on the . . . campus among the students about why should that minority of people [blacks] be able to tell us that we can't play 'Dixie'. . . . And yet we were able to see that that was an absolute insult to the dignity of . . . a certain group of people. It was a very small thing really to give up . . . to show that we were going to try to learn and respect all people. ❞

Although in retrospect the tensions between the races on campus may not have been so serious as many authorities believed at the time, the former SGA president had not forgotten the anxieties of that momentous year. Pierce was constantly called upon to moderate flaring tempers. One white fraternity, Kappa Alpha, insisted upon wearing Confederate uniforms and sporting the flag of the extinct Rebel republic. "I remember there were problems there," Pierce understated. When angry black students followed up a football game with acts of vandalism in one of the dormitories, the student executive anticipated "a real brawl" on the following night. Campus authorities persuaded Pierce to swear out a peace bond against several black activists. When Pierce followed this questionable advice, he did not realize that he would be responsible for delivering the document to the black student leaders. "I can't believe I did that," reflected

Pierce. "That was really dumb." While Pierce made a sincere effort to keep open the lines of communication between the SGA and the blacks—"'dialogue' was the big word"—the SGA was, in the eyes of the blacks, merely an "arm of the administration."

Perhaps the most important development in the early 1970s for the black population served by ASU was the employment of blacks in the faculty and administration. The first of these was Calvin Smith, who became an instructor of history in 1970. Smith recognized that when the university employed him, as well as other blacks, the administration was doing what was strategic. "I knew why I was hired anyway," he added. "I knew the whole State of Arkansas was under pressure to hire black faculty members." F. Clark Elkins, academic vice president, was frank with the new employee. "He told me that they were under pressure to hire" a black. Yet Smith also believed that his presence on the ASU faculty had been a real boon to the black population in Arkansas:

66 When I took the job, I told my wife 'It's going to be a challenge to me to go into that situation.' And I feel that since I've been successful in that situation, it may have led people in the administration to feel that others could possibly be successful if given the opportunity. . . . Somebody has to break the ice. 99

As the university searched for a new identity in the late 1960s and early 1970s, this quest took many forms. One area that developed a new feeling of solidarity was the student body. Its elected spokesman, the Student Government Association, assumed an independent attitude and expressed its feelings for the campus in a novel way. When a local radio station, KBTM, persisted in broadcasting Razorback football games at the same time that ASU was playing home games, Pierce and his colleagues determined to convey their displeasure. In an imaginative take-off on the popular televison program, *Laugh-In* with its "Fickle Finger of Fate" award, the SGA presented the "Heavy Hatchet of Hate" to Alan Patteson, owner of the radio station, and the broadcast's sponsors. Patteson

The late 1960s and early 1970s saw championship seasons in baseball. The Indians won Southland Conference Championships in 1967, 1968, and 1970. The Indians were NCAA Mid-West Regional Champions in 1967 and 1968 and were third in the College Division World Series in 1968.

good-naturedly responded with a container of "Razorback sow milk," which, he claimed (in Pierce's words), was "rich in all of these vitamins." Although it is difficult to conclude who emerged second best in this humorous incident, the fact remained that the ASU student body was revealing a growing solidarity typical of a university campus.

This search for university identity extended into all areas of campus life. Ike Tomlinson broadened the activities of the athletic department, and the football team won new stature in the late 1960s under head coach Bennie Ellender. In three consecutive seasons—1968, 1969, and 1970—the Indians played in the Pecan Bowl, an honor for college division teams. The victory over Drake University (Des Moines, Iowa) in the 1969 Pecan Bowl was an especially memorable one. Bill Davidson, an assistant to Ellender, recalled that the event began ominously when a Drake player knocked the starting quarterback James Hamilton out of the game. ASU was up to the challenge. "We bring [in] a little quarterback named Bubba Crockett," recalled Davidson proudly, "and he wins the outstanding player trophy for the ballgame." The Indians won 29-21. In the following season, ASU not only beat Central Missouri in the Pecan Bowl, but the 11-0 season elevated the Indians into the position of national champions in the college division.

The man who guided the football team to three Pecan Bowls defied the stereotypical image of the coach. Bennie Ellender was quiet, almost meek, and always a gentleman. Davidson recalled this mild-mannered man fondly:

66 He was a slowed-down, honest guy [and] one of the most respected people in the coaching profession. . . . He was really a gentleman. It wasn't false, so it worked. . . . It worked with his players the same way. They knew that he was sincere and honest. 99

The reputation that Bennie Ellender earned at ASU took him to the position of head coach at Tulane University.

Upon the departure of Ellender in 1971, Bill Davidson, the former assistant, assumed the post

Hurdler Thomas Hill (above left) represented ASU—and the United States—at the 1972 Olympics in Munich, West Germany. He came home with the Bronze Medal.

One of ASU's most outstanding athletes, Bill Bergey (above right), was voted first team All-America in 1968 by the Associated Press and the American Football Coaches Association. He was named to the Southland Conference's All-First Decade Team and was voted top player in ASU history by a special poll of fans in 1976. Bergey went on to play with the Cincinnati Bengals and the Philadelphia Eagles. He was named All-Pro in 1974, 1976, 1977, and 1978.

A dejected football coach Bill Davidson (right) leaves the field after a disappointing defeat. During the 1960s and 1970s, the Indian football teams attained national ranking several times.

Dana Ryan (left), named to the college division All-America team in 1967, later played professional baseball. Since World War II, twenty-three Indians have signed pro baseball contracts.

of head football coach. Davidson's first years were difficult. Losing seasons were common. The coach recalled those trying times when, during a particularly poor performance, he would say to himself, "Hell, we're terrible; we're fired!" But just as suddenly, an unexpected event would spark the team out of its lethargy. In the 1973 season, recalled Davidson, a junior college transfer, Willie Harris, "ran the kick-off back and . . . ignited a bunch of just average football players." The team won seven games in that season and duplicated this record the next year.

As the Reng presidency drew to a close in 1975, ASU demonstrated substantial signs of progress as an university. At the same time, some outmoded patterns of thinking remained from ASU's college days. Yet the faculty and the administration had taken those first laborious steps, and the university continued to perform the important functions of teaching, research, and service through all these growing pains.

From Reng's point of view, the principal purpose of the university was "to promote the educational welfare of the state . . . to surround them [students] with the kind of educational programs and the type of faculty members and the library and the books where they will grow and develop into the kind of citizens we'd like." The university was making great strides toward the accomplishment of that mission.

Construction of a new athletic complex, including an 18,000-seat football stadium, heralded a new effort to achieve national recognition.

Head coach Bennie Ellender led the football Indians to national prominence on the gridiron in the late 1960s and early 1970s.

CHAPTER VII

"IT KEPT GETTING BETTER ALL THE TIME"

A Period of Maturation

The mid-seventies began a period of changes in leadership. Ross Pritchard (top) succeeded Carl Reng as president of ASU in 1975. In 1978 Carl Whillock (above right) assumed the presidency. He left in 1980 to enter the private sector. Ray Thornton (above, with medallion) served as president from 1980 to 1984, when he turned over the reins of leadership to Eugene Smith (lower right).

When Carl R. Reng retired from the presidency of Arkansas State in 1975, the youthful university entered a period of unsettling, but productive transition similar to that following V.C. Kays' retirement from a long tenure as president in 1943. Just as the eight years between the successful Kays and Reng administrations were filled with the short terms of Thompson and Edens, a similar quick rotation followed Reng's retirement. Three chief executives, Ross Pritchard, Carl Whillock, and Ray Thornton, led the institution before Eugene W. Smith, who had served an interim term in 1980, became president. While the decade following the departure of Reng exhibited similarities to the unsettled 1940s, a definite but less apparent difference prevailed. In the years 1943-51, the effects of war and changes in the college administration contributed to instability. Yet the same kind of potentially weakening forces from 1975 to 1984 failed to slow the process of growth.

Mark Lewis, 1980-81 Student Government Association president, observed firsthand the impact of the administrative changes on the student body. His class entered ASU during the final year of the Pritchard administration, attended during the entire Whillock presidency and the Smith interim period, and graduated at the end of Thornton's first year in office. Lewis recalled:

❝ In general the students probably didn't detect a whole lot of differences between administrations. . . . (But) I think they maybe to a little bit of a degree really questioned whether ASU would be on an upward progression due to the different presidents. . . . The change in administrations seemed to always worry people a little bit because they felt like everything started at Day One every time a new president came in. **"**

Despite any concern, Lewis believed that the university continued to show obvious signs of growth. By this time, the institution had gathered a momentum of its own that was not slowed by changes in the highest office.

Reng's immediate successor, Ross Pritchard, came to northeast Arkansas after a varied career that included playing football as a University of Arkansas undergraduate, earning a Ph.D. in international relations, teaching at Southwestern University at Memphis, conducting an unsuccessful campaign for the United States Congress, serving as an administrator in the Peace Corps, and holding the presidency of Hood College in Maryland. Despite this valuable experience, Pritchard failed to form a supporting coalition among faculty, students, townspeople, and politicians in Little Rock. Eugene Smith concluded that Pritchard's relatively short stay at ASU (he left in 1978) was a consequence of his being Reng's successor:

" It is not unusual, if we look across the country at the long-term presidencies, for that successor not to stay too long. . . . [Moreover], Dr. Pritchard probably inherited the end of the student unrest movement. There was some student dissatisfaction, I think, with at least some of his policies. **"**

Yet Pritchard's presidency produced some discernible results. He brought some refreshing informality to the institution. This was reflected in his style of dress. Smith described the president's typical clothing:

" He was quite informal. I think he was most comfortable in a pair of bright plaid slacks, button-down oxford cloth shirt with no tie, a pair of comfortable loafers and no socks. And he would top that with a sweater or a blue blazer. . . .

He certainly could dress well and make a very dignified appearance. He looked just as well in a pin-stripe as he did informally, but I think he was most comfortable in casual clothes. **"**

Pritchard worked very long hours. Smith characterized his schedule:

" Ross liked to get up early in the morning. He liked to come to work early. It wasn't unusual for him to be in the office by seven o'clock in the morning, and that's when he did, he said, his best work. . . . He, of course, was . . . a world-class athlete. I detected a little bit of the discipline and regimen of that in him: the early rising, the good health, (and) exercise. **"**

Although the Pritchard administration was shortlived, the hard-working executive contributed to the establishment of a new university identity. Smith remembered "his very keen interest in opening the university's opportunities for minorities." By the 1980s, about ten percent of the student enrollment was black, largely as a result of aggressive recruiting during Pritchard's administration. In addition, blacks occupied faculty and top-level administrative positions on campus.

Pritchard also desired to open "more avenues for faculty input into institutional decision-making," as Smith said. In fact, Pritchard, his staff, and faculty representatives drafted a faculty handbook that clearly increased faculty participation in the governance of the university. The handbook resolved much of the conflict over faculty contributions to personnel decisions, which had reached a critical point during the years immediately following university status.

In 1978, Carl Whillock became president of ASU. After serving in the Arkansas House of Representatives and as executive secretary to Arkansas Governor David Pryor (now U.S. Senator), Whillock moved into higher education. He was supervising governmental relations at the University of Arkansas at Fayetteville when he was chosen for the ASU presidency. Supporters of the university hoped that Whillock would be able to restore the "era of good relations with

state government," as Eugene Smith put it, which had been lacking during the Pritchard years.

In contrast to the informality of Ross Pritchard, Whillock resumed or initiated many of the academic traditions associated with a university. These included formal faculty receptions, a presidential investiture ceremony, and the establishment of a Convocation of Scholars Week to focus attention on academic accomplishments.

Whillock's major contribution was to define more clearly the institution's missions: teaching, research, and public service. He also arranged a cooperative program with the University of Arkansas through which ASU became an agricultural experiment station, thus improving its research potential. But his time at ASU was brief. He left the university to take a position outside academic life in January 1980.

Mark Lewis viewed Whillock as an able administrator, "someone who takes the wheel and drives the ship." However, Lewis continued:

" The short amount of time there [in the presidency] probably hindered him to a certain degree. I think he probably had some good programs and concerns for the university to see it grow and blossom. And I think that he had the interest of the institution at heart in what he was doing as administrator. **"**

After a six-month interim presidency filled by Smith, Ray Thornton became the seventh president in July 1980. A former state attorney general and United States congressman, Thornton was director of the Joint Educational Consortium, a cooperative effort of Henderson State University, Ouachita Baptist University, and the Ross Foundation of Arkadelphia, Arkansas.

In three and one-half years as president, Thornton introduced new trends and reinforced old ones. He promoted a stronger "international flavor" on the ASU campus by attracting more students from abroad. He re-emphasized the desirability of a broad liberal education for young people and worked to strengthen faculty morale. Furthermore, Thornton's involvement in a new honors program—he personally conducted some classes—impressed upon the university his commitment to excellence. With his statewide, and even national reputation, he broadened the visibility and reputation of Arkansas State University.

Thornton brought some definite thoughts about public and higher education to the campus. In his short tenure, he devoted much energy to the realization of his philosophy of education:

❝ I grew up in a school-teaching family that had the understanding that education was the most important task of a civilization—if by that word . . . you [mean] the life-long task of educing from individuals the special qualities of mind and character which enable them to live as civilized persons in a civilized society. . . . Higher education is based upon bringing out the qualities of inquiry, exploration, and adventure in learning. Earlier [public school] education can be the process of encouraging people to think, but it also is in part programming people in a positive way so they can react to day-to-day problems. And I am very concerned that the programming aspect should not be overemphasized because when a mind is programmed, it can only react to the problems which are anticipated. Far better is a system which teaches a person to analyze and to think carefully. . . . And higher education is an association of people who share that interest in the adventure of the full development of the human mind. **❞**

This maturation of the human mind was not confined to a four-year stay on a university campus, declared Thornton, but should continue indefinitely as "a part of everyday living." Before leaving ASU in 1984, Thornton put his philosophy of education into effect. Mark Lewis asserted that he "geared up the academic side of the school a lot, which gained respect over the state and outside the state." The former SGA president summed up Thornton's point of view as a "philosophy of we're here to educate."

When Eugene Smith assumed the presidency in 1984, he brought to the office a lifetime association with the university and northeast Arkansas. Born in nearby Forrest City, where his father was superintendent of schools, he earned

Fine arts continues to interest many students at ASU. The College of Fine Arts includes art, music, speech, and dramatic arts.

his undergraduate degree at Arkansas State in 1952. After military service, he earned a master's and a doctorate from the University of Mississippi.

Upon his return to Arkansas in 1958, Smith began a permanent relationship with the campus. He served in numerous capacities, the most enduring as dean of the Graduate School and executive vice president. When the board of trustees announced that Smith would succeed the outgoing Ray Thornton on February 15, 1984,

Smith received the applause of northeast Arkansans who had observed and followed the progress of his career for more than two decades. He possessed a profound knowledge of the administrative processes of the campus, as well as the personal characteristics of cordiality, openness, and a methodical and expert style in the performance of his duties.

Lewis, who recalled Smith as a stabilizing force during the earlier interim period, said that

The university responded to national trends by emphasizing high technology in many of its programs.

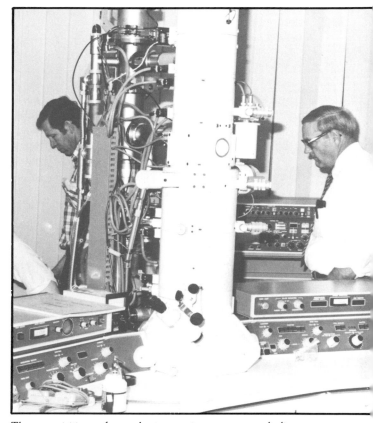

The acquisition of an electron microscope symbolizes ASU's growing commitment to the advancement of science and technology.

the new president's long experience with the school as a student and an administrator should lead to "great things in the future":

&& He's very easy to deal with, very concerned for the students, and I think beyond most things he has a real heart for the development of the school. And his ties with the business community, the Chamber of Commerce, and City Council . . . are just going to be . . . enhancements to the dealings with the community. 🙶

During each of these brief presidencies, the university continued to develop and clarify its role as a center for higher learning and research. New colleges were added and old units were

reorganized to better accommodate the growing student body and to provide for more efficient administration of the campus. In 1979, the board of trustees adopted a campus master plan that provided for the orderly and attractive growth of the 800-acre campus. The Department of Nursing became a college in 1979 and later expanded

into the College of Nursing and Health Professions. The College of Agriculture became the College of Engineering, Agriculture, and Applied Sciences to reflect the expansion of the engineering program beyond the agricultural engineering major and to incorporate programs from the Institute of Technology and Management that had been established by Pritchard. In a major reshuffle, Thornton united the colleges of liberal arts and science to comprise a College of Arts and Sciences.

During this period of growth the museum, which had become nationally accredited in 1973, moved from the lower floor of the Dean B. Ellis Library to a new specially designed facility. An addition to the library enabled it to house its growing holdings and to offer other services. An education-communications building with the latest technological innovations was dedicated with much fanfare in 1983. The legislature authorized construction of a monumental convocation center for special events at an estimated cost of twelve million dollars.

Such elaborate facilities were necessary to handle an ever growing and cosmopolitan student body which, in defiance of all prophecies, reached a record-breaking enrollment of 8,400 in the fall of 1983. The combined student body of the Jonesboro and Beebe campuses approached 10,000. To meet the educational needs of these students, the Jonesboro campus offered fifteen undergraduate degrees in seventy-eight areas and fifteen graduate degrees in fifty-eight areas. Two associate degrees in fourteen areas were offered at Beebe.

While the student body and degree programs at ASU were expanding so strikingly, the administration still took a personal interest in student welfare and, more than ever, respected student opinions on matters affecting the governance of the institution. In fact, one of the most memorable qualities of Ray Thornton as president, in the opinion of Mark Lewis, was the chief executive's good relations with students. Lewis remembered:

❝ He was very open to . . . suggestions and respected your opinion as a representative of the students, regardless of whether it aligned with his opinion of a given situation. . . . There was never a battle between the students and Ray Thornton . . . because you simply put out on the table what you thought and what he thought and tried to compromise and come up with the best solution for the school. . . . There was more than adequate student input on every given situation that I can think of that would have any impact on the students. **❞**

Lewis was particularly impressed with Thornton's scheduling a period of time each day so that students "could come in and just talk to him."

A remarkable increase in the teaching staff was another obvious manifestation of growth as a

Minority students became more and more involved in campus activities. The mid-1970s saw the election of the first all-black homecoming court.

university: from 218 in 1967 at the outset of university status to 405 in 1984. Within the faculty a growing proportion held the doctoral degree. The academic community considered the terminal degree necessary if one wished not only to teach, but to perform the essential research and publication duties of a scholar. This growing faculty also received encouragement to perform these tasks through university research incentives, especially a stronger leave program. The stature of the faculty was measured to some degree by the award of research grants from outside agencies such as the National Science Foundation, the National Endowment for the Humanities, the National Endowment for the Arts, and the Department of Energy. Thornton, who took a keen interest in the welfare of the faculty, sought to strengthen this body through the employment of academics from a wide variety of universities throughout the country. A foreign exchange of faculty also played a part in this program.

In another instance of the broadening of opportunity, the university attempted to serve "non-traditional" students, individuals who were returning to formal education after being part of the regional work force. Of course, the World War II veterans on campus in the late 1940s represented an older, more seasoned student population, and the university had always attracted public school teachers who wished to update their knowledge and techniques. But in the 1970s the university made a more enduring attempt to attract mature students. The Pritchard administration expanded the continuing education program to offer courses of general community interest. Mature persons also found their way into conventional university classrooms. Their motives for seeking a university education were varied. Some wanted to find more lucrative employment, others sought skills that would enhance the performance of their present jobs, and others were simply bent on learning. One of these last was Walter Grundon, an octogenarian and pioneering rice farmer who enrolled in some history courses in 1982 as one of the school's oldest students:

❝ I'm interested in learning all I can about everything. I'd studied history back in high

The ASU Museum found a permanent home in an impressive facility adjoining the library and broadened its role on campus. Eugene and Elizabeth Wittlake were honored for their many years of service at the museum's re-opening.

Exhibits in the ASU Museum include natural history, Indian cultures, pioneer history, military history, foreign cultures, toys, and the glass collection.

During the 1970s the university placed greater emphasis on its research function. The addition of the Cass S. Hough Aeronautical Collection provided opportunities for specialized study and research in the Dean B. Ellis Library.

Education professor Mildred Vance was ASU's first Faculty Member of the Year in 1979. The award became a highlight of the annual Convocation of Scholars Week.

Carl Whillock, with Arkansas Governor Bill Clinton, wears the university's new medallion at his 1979 investiture. This traditional badge of office is worn by the president at official academic ceremonies.

The mace, carried for the first time at Ray Thornton's investiture in 1981, was presented to the university by Arkansas Gamma Chapter of Sigma Phi Epsilon. Originally a weapon of the Middle Ages, the mace is carried as a symbol of presidential authority.

school, but never gave it a thought all during the years. 🙶

As the institution continued to seek an identity in the years after 1967, it routinely sought students from beyond the boundaries of its limited constituency in Jonesboro and northeast Arkansas. During Thornton's tenure, students living within a seventy-five mile radius of Jonesboro, but beyond the state line, were permitted to pay in-state tuition rather than the increasingly higher out-of-state rates.

Efforts of the university to expand went beyond state and even national boundaries to include students from throughout the world. More and more frequently, international students were visible on campus. Although ASU had attracted such students since the 1930s when Tin Boo Yee studied on the campus, not until Thornton's presidency did the university make a concerted effort to import a cosmopolitan flavor. As he explained, his first desire was to promote a wide representation of nationalities in the student body:

🙶 Every student that comes to Arkansas State University, whether it's from Poughkeepsie or Newport or Lake City, [should have] . . . the opportunity of interacting with people of different cultures and different backgrounds, and that is the next best thing to world travel in order to understand the nature of the world. And it is an enriching part of our university campus. It has added . . . to the overall enrichment that I would count as the primary achievement of my being here. 🙶

The most significant international presence consisted of the Saudi Arabians, who came to northeast Arkansas through a contract between the university and the United States Customs Service. In the early 1970s the Saudi Arabian government contracted with the United States to receive computer, technological, and other training in this country. One feature of this agreement focused on the Saudi Customs Service. Since Saudi Arabia imports much of its consumer needs, and since many Moslems make pilgrimages to the sacred places of Islam located there, the Saudi customs service must manage a significant flow of goods and people. The United

States Customs Service agreed to assist the Saudis in modernizing their customs procedures and subcontracted in 1981 with Arkansas State University to provide this training program. The arrangement resulted largely from pleasant experiences that other Saudi students not connected with the customs program had at ASU.

With the arrival of numerous Saudi Arabian customs officials and their families (as well as a sizeable body of Malaysian and Nigerian students), citizens of Jonesboro had to adjust to the presence of these many guests. Thornton and his assistants were somewhat concerned that the community might hesitate to accept them:

" Any time you try something new or different you must necessarily be concerned about how that will impact on the community, and consequently it was with some nervousness that we started some of these major [international] programs, knowing that if the community . . . didn't like it, it could really bring the programs down pretty quickly. The success of the programs depended upon the students being warmly received by the community. **"**

The response of Jonesboroans could not have been more positive. Thornton added:

" I have never seen anything better than the way the City of Jonesboro, Craighead County, and the surrounding counties have received these international students. They've opened their homes to them, programs have been developed for foreign students to spend vacations with families as 'adopted' students. The students have been welcomed in the stores [and] business areas of town. . . . There really was among the city officials and the church groups and the leaders among the community a warm reception for these international programs. **"**

The uneasiness of the university executive was a natural condition. Each of three successive generations of Jonesboroans have observed the growth of ASU with some trepidation. The presence of this institution of higher education represents, at once, an economic blessing and the

ASU took on an international flavor in the eighties with the establishment of a U.S.-Saudi Arabian program to provide training for customs officials.

The influx of international students brought a cosmopolitan atmosphere to events such as the annual Spring Festival. Forty countries were represented on the ASU campus in the 1980s.

President Ray Thornton took a personal interest in the establishment of an Honors Program and served as part of a three-member teaching team for one of its first inter-disciplinary courses.

Bob Hope performed at an ASU concert in the mid-seventies and visited with T.J. Humphreys, a first-team football All-American.

threat of new ideas. In the long run it appears that the community has warmed to this imposing corporate body.

When Donald Minx arrived from Indiana in the 1950s, he found that the citizenry regarded ASU as their "college" and resented any demands that neighboring communities made upon the limited resources of the campus. He remembered that they thought of it as "Jonesboro College" and cited an instance of the community's possessiveness:

❝ The college band always had to go to downtown Jonesboro to play for the Christmas parade. Well, I thought as a civic function, we are part of the community and all, and yet when other people began to say to me, 'Hey, Don, this isn't Jonesboro College. How about coming to Paragould to play, to Walnut Ridge, Pocahontas, to one place and another?' Then we had to draw a line some place. Then I became aware of the fact that, yeah, this isn't Jonesboro College. Yet at the same time I think it is one of those relationships between the college and the city where you probably do a little more here than you do in another town because we are here together and need to have a compatible relationship. **❞**

But Minx, who served on the Jonesboro City Council, emphasized that as the university grew and expanded, its relationship with Jonesboro continually improved.

Dannye Pierce, who graduated from ASU in 1970, has observed the progress of town-gown relations for more than a decade from the perspective of a businessman:

❝ When I was a student, I thought the City of Jonesboro didn't appreciate ASU. Now that I'm a businessman, I think probably that the city . . . is just awfully good in their support of ASU. Now, I think sometimes they don't understand [the nature of university affairs], . . . and sometimes their comments are a little misguided, but generally I think that Jonesboro supports ASU. **❞**

Participation in the Olympic Games in the seventies enhanced ASU's athletic reputation. Track coach Guy Kochel (left in photo at right) and former Olympian Tom Hill (center) assist 1976 Olympic team member Ed Preston at an ASU track meet.

ASU athletes Al Joyner (left) and Earl Bell represented the university well in the 1984 Olympic Games in Los Angeles. Joyner won the gold medal in the triple jump and Bell took the bronze medal in the pole vault.

During the 1970s the athletic program at ASU offered a broad range of intercollegiate sports, including women's basketball and fencing.

Fraternities and sororities are a major source of annual extra curricular activities. Zeta Tau Alpha sorority raises money through an annual talent show, and Sigma Phi Epsilon fraternity encourages intramural competition at its Fite Nite.

More and more frequently ASU students moved from the dormitories into apartments in Jonesboro.

Women's intercollegiate volleyball was initiated at ASU in 1975. The record-setting Tomahawks won 97 straight Arkansas Women's Intercollegiate Sports Association conference matches before the program was elevated to Division I status in the NCAA.

...sident Ray Thornton was one of several colorfully ...umed participants in the first Renaissance festival, ...ed in 1983.

The Department of Military Science broadened its offerings to include practical skills such as rappelling and riflery and attracted female as well as male cadets.

While the university sought new sources of students in faraway places, the administration continued to strengthen ASU's offerings to its immediate service area. The engineering program was re-emphasized by offering a bachelor of science in engineering degree in addition to agricultural engineering. Thornton declared that the new program was "a very real responsibility to the community":

❝ Engineering is one area where Arkansas has had great difficulty in attracting and keeping the quality of engineers, especially in eastern Arkansas, that our communities need. An engineer often stays in the area where he or she is educated. A person goes to Georgia Tech and gets an engineering degree, [and] most likely will stay in either Georgia or one of the surrounding states. . . . We thought that the best way to meet the demands for engineers in eastern Arkansas was to . . . get that education located here. **❞**

The business and industrial community—potential employers of newly graduated engineers—provided invaluable services as the university sought permission to offer the new degree. Said Thornton:

❝ We got enormous support from the [Association of] Existing Industries of Northeast Arkansas in analyzing the needs for engineers—in making the case that we were not competing with the engineering program 200 miles away [in Fayetteville], but rather with engineering programs in Tennessee, Missouri, and Mississippi which were siphoning off the capable minds of eastern Arkansas. . . . We were able with their help and with the best community support I've ever seen to persuade the State Board of Higher Education. **❞**

This community support also contributed to the growth of the athletic program and facilities. Coach Richard Johnson, with much voluntary public assistance, gave the Kell Field baseball diamond a facelift. An ultra-modern training, office, and dressing room facility was added to the southern approach to Indian Stadium. Such modern facilities for athletics astounded football coach Bill Davidson, who was accustomed to

make-do and minimal resources. Before moving into the new office quarters, he and his staff occupied two small house trailers that private benefactors made available. Davidson reflected upon the confining effects of these skimpy facilities:

ASU defied national trends by increasing enrollment in the early eighties. Registrar Greta Mack (right) greets Lisa Spriggs, ASU's 8,000th student to register in the fall of 1983.

❝ My whole head-coaching career was in those trailers. There's not enough time or my vocabulary won't allow me to . . . explain to you just how those trailers functioned. The person who had claustrophobia was in trouble. That's why I had the sliding glass door right in front of my desk. Every now and then I had to break and run. I had to get out of there. 🙶

In Davidson's thinking, the dedication of the new Indian Stadium in the 1974 football season launched ASU's athletic program into a new era. The old Kays Stadium accommodated 5,000 spectators; the new facility seated more than 18,000. Architects designed the structure so that additional seating could be added. The coach claimed that the athletic complex provided coaches with the opportunity to recruit better athletes:

🙶 Today when high school seniors [visit] our campus and see this facility, they're impressed with it. I think it gives us an edge now that we didn't have. 🙶

In 1975 ASU won a place in the much-coveted Division I of the National Collegiate Athletic Association, a promotion that placed the Indians alongside the strongest athletic programs of the major universities. Since that time, the Indians have experienced both triumph and defeat. They concluded the 1975 season victoriously and, like Bennie Ellender's 1970 team, were undefeated. While Davidson remembered this aggregation fondly, he recalled other seasons more clearly. "The fans remember the '75 [team]," said the veteran coach, but "the things that stand out in your mind are the games that you didn't win."

The pressures of being head football coach were unrelenting, and the rigors of preparing for a big game often manifested themselves in bizarre ways. Superstitions became a part of Davidson's preparation process. Failure to abide by a certain ritual could cost the Indians a game in the coach's thinking. In the triumphant 1975 season, Davidson had to keep his bulldog puppy with him at all times. On another occasion, he had to eat liver with friends on Thursdays. Baseball coach Richard Johnson had to attend every football game during one season. Perhaps Davidson's most time-consuming superstition had to do with his belief that encountering a red light would mean a touchdown for the opposition:

Indian Stadium has been the pride of ASU football since its inauguration with the 1974 season. The double-decked west side contains a four-level press box for premium boosters and news media.

ABC-TV came to Indian Stadium in 1979 for a regionally televised game. In the last decade, television exposure has become essential to the growth of the football program.

167

Students haven't changed much over the past seventy-five years in their ideas of a good time.

"I have driven every possible way that you can drive from here to . . . [my home by] different routes. I tried to stay away from red lights. I have every one of them figured out on time. I knew if I could make this one, then this [one]. . . . If some guy would get in front of me, I'd just exit off here and take . . . another one [street]. It was red lights in my mind that were touchdowns. . . . So that meant that I had to score . . . greens."

When Bill Davidson left the position of head coach after the 1978 season, Larry Lacewell assumed the post. Lacewell set out to improve the schedule of games so the Indians would engage stronger teams on the gridiron. His efforts proved successful, including even a highly publicized match-up in 1982 with the University of Alabama, the team of the highly lauded coach, Paul "Bear" Bryant.

While a number of new academic programs were added in the late 1970s and early 1980s, the university also revised or modified traditional ones. For decades ASU had maintained a steadfast allegiance to the notion of a set of basic education (general) requirements for all incoming students. With few exceptions, students devoted their freshman and sophomore years to fulfillment of these requirements. And while some members of the faculty desired the relaxation or removal of this general education curriculum, Thornton maintained that such a program was essential to the production of the well-rounded citizen. Another term for this general education program was "liberal education." As Thornton explained:

"Liberal . . . 'to liberate' . . . means 'to set free' . . . to set a mind free from the constraints that limit the ability of that mind to achieve. And, in that sense, a liberal education is at the core of every professional."

The president's desire for the continuation of this general education requirement was confirmed in 1983 when a special committee, with the task of re-examining this curriculum, reaffirmed the university's commitment to a liberal education. Although some modifications were made in the program, the body of freshman and sophomore courses remained largely intact. As Thornton recalled, the unification of the colleges of liberal arts and science the preceding fall represented another effort to strengthen the notion of liberal education.

Although a well-educated student has been the primary goal of the university, the maintenance of this largely intangible ideal is always difficult. One measure of a university's performance is the maintenance of high academic standards. Edgar Kirk, who attended ASC as a student in the 1930s and returned to serve in the history department for twenty years, expressed the sentiments of the academic community regarding quality education:

"The quality of education here is something that I have always been interested in. As I was a student here and then as I was away teaching in high school and observing the college from a distance, then after I came back here to teach, I always had the desire to see more emphasis put on quality of education, not meaning to imply that we have had no quality in the early days. I found no difficulty whatever when I went from here to graduate school [at the University of Arkansas]. I think it prepared me as well as those I was with from larger and better known schools."

Local businessman Lloyd Langford, speaking perhaps for many citizens of Jonesboro, stated:

"We were interested in seeing Arkansas State grow. Which it has done. I sometimes think that it's outgrown us in the city of Jonesboro. Which goes to prove that you can't stand in the way of progress when education is involved."

Retired faculty member Warren W. Nedrow reflected on the changes on campus during the last half-century:

"It kept getting better all the time. . . . [I said when I came], 'I think things are going to grow.' And boy, have we seen it grow!"

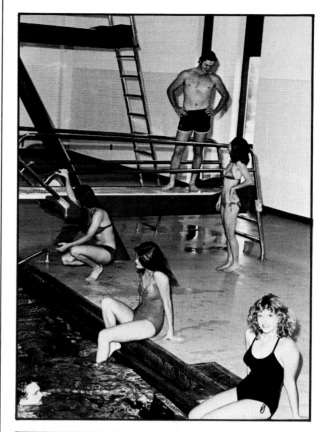

The physical education complex, located west of the jogging track, was completed in 1975. It includes general and specialized areas for indoor archery, wrestling, and dance; an auditorium; handball courts; swimming pool; locker facilities; sauna; and two gymnasiums.

The convocation center, designed to seat about 10,000 people, is one of the most ambitious construction projects undertaken by ASU. When completed (as this model shows), the facility will cover a city block.

Robert E. Lee Wilson III, member of an eastern Arkansas family that has supported A-State generously throughout its 75-year history, received an honorary doctorate from the institution at the 1982 commencement. John A. Cooper, Sr. also received an honorary doctorate at the 1982 ceremonies.

Herbert Hall McAdams II was awarded the honorary Doctor of Laws Degree during spring 1984 commencement exercises. Conferring the degree are President Eugene Smith (left) and Board of Trustees Chairman Richard Herget. McAdams was one of the founders of the Arkansas State University Foundation and has served on the foundation board since its inception.

This 1982 aerial view of the Arkansas State University campus, looking north from the railroad tracks, shows the new education-communications complex to the right of the jogging track and the library and museum addition north of the track.

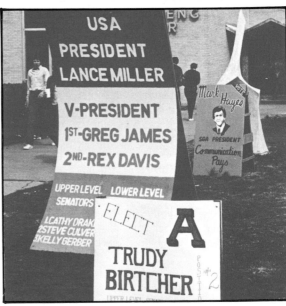

Contending parties waged energetic campaigns for positions in student government as students became increasingly involved in influencing ASU policy.

When the State Agricultural School at Jonesboro was established in 1909, its primary focus was to educate young men and women for an agricultural livelihood. Although by the 1980s the College of Engineering, Agriculture, and Applied Sciences was but one of several branches of the university, ASU still maintained its focus on the region's most important economic pursuit. In many respects the most important measure of the institution's success in carrying out its fundamental charge can be observed in what it has done for agriculture in northeast Arkansas and surrounding areas. Most people believe that it has carried out that charge effectively. John Miller, who participated in and observed agricultural developments in the region for over half a century, commented:

❝ I would say that the progress has been tremendous, making farming a business. Used to [be] it was a livelihood when I was on the farm. . . . The main thing we did was try to raise something to eat and a little cotton to sell, and that was about it. Cotton was about the only marketable thing that we had, you see. And, of course, we didn't grow any cattle. Hogs weren't worth much. . . . You see there how the market has changed, how the livestock prices [have] changed. **❞**

William Wyatt, the former student, faculty member, and board member, also concluded that changes in agriculture were attributable in part at least to the influence of ASU:

❝ Our farmers have looked to Arkansas State, and since they're working now with the research people more and with the experiment stations, they are all trying to work together. It's going to be a big advantage in the future. I think this is one of the best things that the state and the university have done in getting together . . . on their agriculture projects and agriculture courses. **❞**

Yet the institution's influence has extended much beyond its original agricultural focus. More than 30,000 persons have completed academic degree programs from the school. Most people in northeast Arkansas have been touched in some

way by ASU. Many people could offer testimony about the role that the institution—State Agricultural School, First District Agricultural and Mechanical College, Arkansas State College, and then Arkansas State University—has played in their lives. If ASU succeeds in carrying out its new identity as effectively as it did its past identities as high school, junior college, and senior college, it will remain an institution of immense value to the Mid-South.

Members of the first four-year graduating class celebrated their fiftieth anniversary at the 1982 homecoming. Left to right are Dean of Students Robert Moore, Sister Theresina Grob, Lenita Stack, Ottoleine Detrick Echols, Allie Hiett Dunkling, Margaret Warr Winters Wall, Gertrude Love Plunkett, and President Ray Thornton.

171

Although the university campus has been completely transformed, the traditions exemplified by the early gateway to Aggie remind students and visitors of the university's seventy-five-year heritage.

ASU CAMPUS MAP

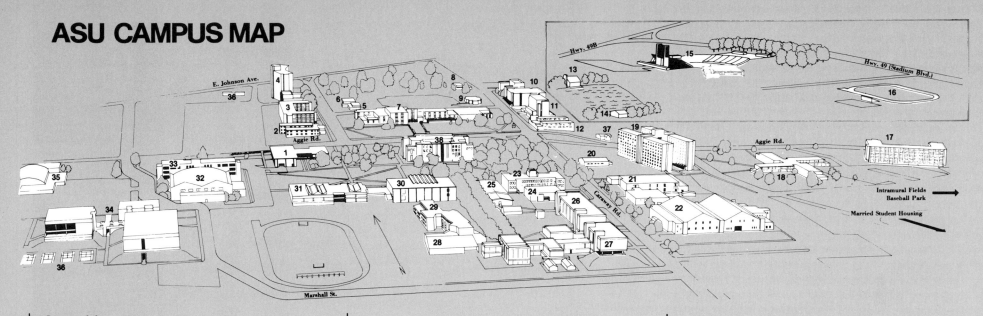

Legend for campus map:

1. Administration Building
2. Saudi Arabian Center
3. University Hall (Women's Residence)
4. Kays Hall (Women's Residence)
5. Wesley Foundation
6. Church of Christ Center
7. Carl R. Reng Center
8. Baptist Student Center
9. Wilson Student Health Center
10. Student Services Center
11. Nursing and Health Professions
12. Indian Hall (Men's Residence)
13. New Student Pavilion
14. Old Student Pavilion
15. Stadium Complex
16. Track Complex
17. Arkansas Hall (Women's Residence)
18. Delta Hall (Men's Residence)
19. Seminole Twin Towers
    (Men's Residence)
20. Post Office (State University, AR 72467)
21. Fine Arts Center
22. Physical Plant
23. Old Education Building

24. Art Annex
25. Computer Services Center
26. Laboratory Science Center
27. Agriculture/Engineering Center
28. Communications
29. Education
30. Dean B. Ellis Library
31. Continuing Education Center
32. Field House
33. Business
34. Physical Education Complex
35. Military Science, ROTC
36. Tennis Courts
37. Campus Security
38. Wilson Hall

As Arkansas State University celebrates its seventy-fifth anniversary, it looks forward to continued growth and development. The university's advancement can only be furthered by the continued support of alumni and friends. To participate in the growth of Arkansas State University through financial giving or other forms of assistance, please contact the ASU Foundation, Inc., P.O. Box 1980, State University, Arkansas 72467.

Arkansas State University is an equal opportunity institution and will not discriminate on the basis of race, color, religion, sex, national origin, age, handicap, or other unlawful factors in employment practices or admission and treatment of students. Any questions regarding this policy should be addressed to the Coordinator of Equal Opportunity and Affirmative Action, Arkansas State University, P.O. Box 2100, State University, Arkansas 72467. Telephone (501) 972-3454.

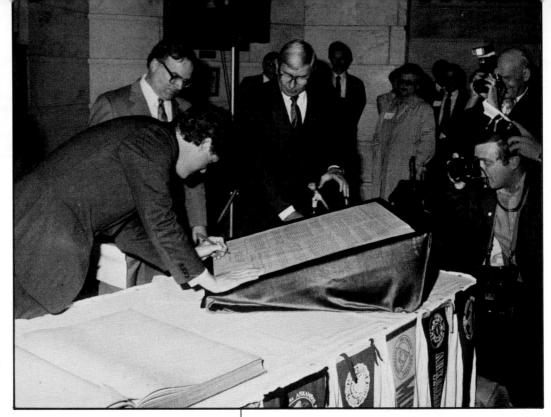

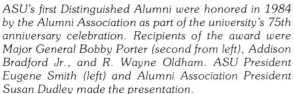

ASU's first Distinguished Alumni were honored in 1984 by the Alumni Association as part of the university's 75th anniversary celebration. Recipients of the award were Major General Bobby Porter (second from left), Addison Bradford Jr., and R. Wayne Oldham. ASU President Eugene Smith (left) and Alumni Association President Susan Dudley made the presentation.

The Arkansas State University Seal was adopted by the Board of Trustees on March 9, 1979. The university had previously used an adaptation of the seal of the State of Arkansas, which had been modified over the years. The new seal, designed by Roxi Heckmann, a graphic artist on the university's public relations staff, is representative of the university and its principles. The three torches which dominate the design represent ASU's commitment to teaching, research, and service. The torches also resemble diamonds, symbolizing quality of education. The seal contains the inscription "1909" denoting the year the university was founded.

Governor Bill Clinton signs a reproduction of Act 100 of 1909, the act which established Arkansas State University. The signing took place at ceremonies in the State Capitol Rotunda on April 2, 1984, and served as one of the events to begin the university's 75th anniversary celebration.

New television facilities at ASU are among the finest in the nation. Students broadcast daily over the local cable TV system to gain experience with the latest technology.

The new pavilion near the football stadium serves as the focal point for student social gatherings.

APPENDIX A

LIST OF INTERVIEWEES

Fred Barnett (September 20, 1979) attended Aggie during its first decade and was later a businessman in Jonesboro.

Robert Fulton Barnett (June 26, 1979) was a businessman in Jonesboro when the State Agricultural School was formed.

Phil Bridger (December 4, 1979) attended the Arkansas State College Training School, graduated from ASC, and later became chief housing officer at ASU.

Linual Cameron (September 26, 1979; October 3, 1979) attended Arkansas State College during the 1930s and was the institution's chief financial officer during the 1950s and 1960s.

Lebelva Connelly (September 19, 1979) taught at the Arkansas State College Training School and then in the A-State English department.

Paul Couch (October 15, 1979) headed the education department at ASC and was the first director of the institution's graduate programs.

Lou Couch (October 15, 1979) joined her husband in supervising a men's dormitory during the late 1940s.

Nelson Crum (October 16, 1979) attended Aggie during and shortly after World War I.

Bill Davidson (August 22, 1983) attended Arkansas State College in the 1950s and later became head football coach and assistant athletic director.

Clyde Duncan (October 16, 1979) was active on the Aggie campus between 1919 and 1923.

Ottoleine Detrick Echols (January 31, 1983) was a member of the first four-year graduating class at Arkansas State College in 1932.

Max Edens (January 31, 1980) attended ASC just before World War II broke out.

Harry E. "Cap" Eldridge (October 8, 1979) served the institution in a variety of ways—registrar, engineering instructor, National Guard unit commander, and superintendent of the physical plant among others—beginning in the early 1920s.

Lillian Eldridge (October 8, 1979) taught at the training school in the late 1920s.

Forrest W. "Frosty" England (April 23, 1983) was head football coach at Arkansas State College from 1946 to 1953.

Robert Ferralasco (December 10, 1979; December 17, 1979) attended ASC in the late 1940s and later became chairman of the Department of Information Systems and Business Education.

John A. Galloway (November 15, 1979) joined the history faculty of Arkansas State in the late 1940s.

Jane McBride Gates (January 28, 1983) graduated from ASU in 1969 and became one of the first black women faculty members at Arkansas State University.

Walter W. Grundon (July 28, 1983) was a pioneer rice farmer who returned to formal education at ASU when in his eighties.

Ray Hall (November 27, 1979) headed up the field services division of the institution beginning in the 1950s.

Gladys Hudgins (February 2, 1983) took extension courses offered by ASC in the 1940s and later joined the physical education staff.

Jasper "Jap" Hunter (May 24, 1979) served on the institution's physical plant staff from 1935 to 1982.

Victor H. "Buddy" Kays (August 13, 1980; August 18, 1980; August 22, 1980; August 26, 1980) grew up on the Aggie campus during the 1920s and 1930s.

E. Roy Keller (October 18, 1979) was a student at the State Agricultural School during the 1910s.

Edgar Kirk (September 6, 1979; September 13, 1979) attended ASC during the 1930s and later joined the history faculty.

Cleveland Kohonke (May 22, 1979) attended Arkansas State College in the late 1920s and early 1930s.

Eleanor Lane (September 5, 1979), a student at ASC during the 1930s, was on the English faculty for many years.

Lloyd L. Langford (November 7, 1979) went to Aggie during the 1930s and later became a Jonesboro businessman.

Mark Lewis (June 2, 1984) was president of the Student Government Association at ASU in 1980-81.

William Troy Martin (May 24, 1980) attended Aggie at its very beginnings and was on the faculty in the late teens.

Marshall Matthews (September 26, 1979), who attended ASC during the Depression years, became a mathematics instructor.

Elmer Mayes (October 17, 1979) joined the science faculty at his alma mater, which he had attended in the 1930s.

Homer E. McEwen, Jr. (February 15, 1983) grew up on the Aggie campus and completed four years of college at the institution in the late 1930s.

Joyce Lichtenberger McEwen (February 15, 1983) attended ASC before and during World War II and serves on the ASU staff.

John Miller (October 23, 1979) was a student at Aggie during the early 1920s.

Donald Minx (November 6, 1979; November 12, 1979) was band director at the institution beginning in the 1950s and became chairman of the music department.

Robert Moore (May 23, 1979) joined the administrative staff in 1949 and served as dean of students at Arkansas State University.

Olen Nail (October 11, 1979) was first dean of ASU's College of Agriculture.

Lula Nedrow (June 28, 1983) held several positions on the A-State campus, including cafeteria manager.

Warren W. Nedrow (June 28, 1983) came to Arkansas State College in the late 1930s to serve as head of the biology department.

Dannye Pierce (April 19, 1984), president of the Student Government Association at ASU in 1969-70, is a Jonesboro businessman and member of the State Board of Higher Education.

Leland W. "Tex" Plunkett (September 24, 1979; September 27, 1979) was affiliated with the institution as student and faculty member for more than forty years.

Charles Rasberry (February 9, 1983) graduated from ASC in 1956 and joined the communications faculty in 1961.

Carl R. Reng (December 5, 1979) served as president of the institution from 1951 to 1975.

C. Calvin Smith (January 12, 1983) did graduate work at Arkansas State University in the late 1960s and was the first black faculty member at ASU.

Eugene W. Smith (December 12, 1979; August 29, 1983) graduated from ASC in 1952 and served in a number of administrative capacities before becoming the institution's eighth president.

W.L. Smith (November 30, 1979) established the audiovisual program at Arkansas State College.

Lenita Stack (February 10, 1983) was a member of 1932's first four-year class at ASC.

Walter Strong (March 16, 1983) was the institution's first black graduate.

Ray Thornton (January 27, 1984) was ASU's seventh president.

J.A. "Ike" Tomlinson (October 1, 1979; October 2, 1979) came to Arkansas State in 1943, where he chaired the physical education and athletic departments.

Mildred Vance (December 12, 1979), an ASC student during the 1930s, became professor of elementary education.

Wanda Walker (December 12, 1979) taught at the ASC Training School and later in the English department. (Now Mrs. Travis Keahey.)

Margaret Warr Winters Wall (September 10, 1979), a 1932 four-year graduate of the institution, worked as a secretary to President V.C. Kays.

Archer Wheatley (February 8, 1979) was a Jonesboro lawyer who assisted ASC during the 1950s.

Elizabeth Wittlake (June 24, 1983) was assistant director of the ASU Museum.

Eugene B. Wittlake (June 24, 1983), professor of botany, served as director of the ASU Museum.

Mary Grace Wyatt (January 19, 1983) attended Arkansas State in the 1930s.

William Wyatt (January 19, 1983) was affiliated with Arkansas State as student, faculty member, and board member.

APPENDIX B

PHOTO CREDITS

Page 1: William Troy Martin Collection, ASU Museum

Page 2: TOP-Dr. and Mrs. Fred Stull Collection, ASU Museum; BOTTOM LEFT-Courtesy of Fox Studio; BOTTOM RIGHT-William Troy Martin Collection, ASU Museum

Page 3: TOP-Mid-South Center for Oral History; BOTTOM-Courtesy of V.H. Kays

Page 4: TOP-Courtesy of Margaret Wall; BOTTOM LEFT-Courtesy of V.H. Kays; BOTTOM RIGHT-Mid-South Center for Oral History

Page 5: William Troy Martin Collection, ASU Museum

Page 6: TOP-Courtesy of Margaret Wall; BOTTOM-William Troy Martin Collection, ASU Museum

Page 7: William Troy Martin Collection, ASU Museum

Page 8: William Troy Martin Collection, ASU Museum

Page 9: William Troy Martin Collection, ASU Museum

Page 10: William Troy Martin Collection, ASU Museum

Page 11: William Troy Martin Collection, ASU Museum

Page 12: William Troy Martin Collection, ASU Museum

Page 13: William Troy Martin Collection, ASU Museum

Page 14: Courtesy of V.H. Kays

Page 15: Mary Rogers Brown Collection, ASU Museum

Page 16: Courtesy of V.H. Kays

Page 17: Courtesy of V.H. Kays

Page 18: William Troy Martin Collection, ASU Museum; BOTTOM-Courtesy of V.H. Kays

Page 19: William Troy Martin Collection, ASU Museum

Page 20-21: ASU Museum

Page 22: TOP-William Troy Martin Collection, ASU Museum; BOTTOM-Courtesy of V.H. Kays

Page 23: William Troy Martin Collection, ASU Museum

Page 24: William Troy Martin Collection, ASU Museum

Page 25: Goodloe Stuck Collection, ASU Museum

Page 26-27: Courtesy of V.H. Kays

Page 28: ASU Yearbook

Page 29: Mid-South Center for Oral History

Page 30: LEFT-ASU News Service; RIGHT-ASU Yearbook

Page 32: Courtesy of V.H. Kays

Page 33: William Troy Martin Collection, ASU Museum

Page 35: TOP-William Troy Martin Collection, ASU Museum; BOTTOM-Dr. Bernice Coffey Collection, ASU Museum

Page 36: William Troy Martin Collection, ASU Museum

Page 37: Courtesy of V.H. Kays

Page 39: Courtesy of V.H. Kays

Page 40: ASU News Service

Page 42: Courtesy of Tin Boo Yee

Page 43: LEFT-Courtesy of V.H. Kays; RIGHT-Courtesy of Mr. and Mrs. Fred Pasmore

Page 44: Courtesy of Tin Boo Yee

Page 45: TOP, MIDDLE RIGHT, BOTTOM-Courtesy of Tin Boo Yee; MIDDLE LEFT-Courtesy of Homer and Joyce McEwen

Page 46: Courtesy of V.H. Kays

Page 47: TOP LEFT-ASU News Service; TOP RIGHT-Courtesy of Tin Boo Yee; BOTTOM LEFT-Courtesy of Tin Boo Yee; BOTTOM RIGHT-Courtesy of Homer and Joyce McEwen

Page 48: Courtesy of V.H. Kays

Page 49: Courtesy of Tin Boo Yee

Page 50: Courtesy of Tin Boo Yee

Page 51: Courtesy of Tin Boo Yee

Page 53: Courtesy of V.H. Kays

Page 54: Courtesy of Tin Boo Yee

Page 55: Courtesy of V.H. Kays

Page 57: Courtesy of Tin Boo Yee

Page 58-59: Courtesy of V.H. Kays

Page 60: Courtesy of Tin Boo Yee

Page 61: Courtesy of Tin Boo Yee

Page 62: Courtesy of Tin Boo Yee

Page 63: Courtesy of Tin Boo Yee

Page 65: Courtesy of E.M. McIlroy

Page 67: ASU Museum

Page 68: Courtesy of V.H. Kays

Page 69: Courtesy of Mrs. Homer Huitt

Page 71: Courtesy of Nanella Langford Chapman

Page 72: Courtesy of Larry Burns

Page 73: Courtesy of Mrs. Homer Huitt

Page 75: Courtesy of Mrs. Homer Huitt

Page 76: ASU News Service

Page 77: TOP-Courtesy of Mrs. Homer Huitt; BOTTOM-Courtesy of Mrs. Paul Couch

Page 78: TOP-Courtesy of Fox Studio; BOTTOM-ASU Museum

Page 79: TOP-ASU Yearbook; BOTTOM-ASU Museum

Page 80: Courtesy of the family of Ivan S. "Cotton" and Maggie Lew Hogue Busby

Page 81: Courtesy of Mrs. Homer Huitt

Page 82: Courtesy of Joanne Dickerson

Page 83: Courtesy of Joanne Dickerson

Page 84: ASU Yearbook

Page 85: ASU Yearbook

Page 86: Courtesy of Homer and Joyce McEwen

Page 87: ASU Yearbook

Page 88: Courtesy of Mr. and Mrs. Fred Pasmore

Page 89: Courtesy of Mr. and Mrs. Fred Pasmore

Page 90: Courtesy of Mrs. Paul Couch

Page 91: ASU Yearbook

Page 93: ASU News Service

Page 94: TOP- ASU News Service; BOTTOM-ASU Museum

Page 95: Courtesy of Mrs. Donald R. Minx

Page 96: Courtesy of Ray H. Hall, Sr.

Page 97: Courtesy of Mildred Vance

Page 98: ASU Yearbook

Page 99: Courtesy of Robert Moore

Page 100: TOP LEFT and RIGHT-ASU Museum; BOTTOM LEFT and RIGHT-Courtesy of Mrs. Homer Huitt

Page 102: Courtesy of Mrs. Homer Huitt

Page 103: LEFT-ASU News Service; TOP and BOTTOM RIGHT-Courtesy of Robert Moore

Page 104: Courtesy of Robert Moore

Page 105: TOP-Department of Military Science; BOTTOM-ASU Museum

Page 106: Courtesy of Robert Moore

Page 107: Courtesy of Robert Moore

Page 108: TOP-Department of Military Science; BOTTOM-Courtesy of Mr. and Mrs. Fred Pasmore

Page 109: ASU News Service

Page 110: TOP-ASU Museum; BOTTOM-Courtesy of Robert Moore

Page 111: Courtesy of Robert Moore

Page 112: Courtesy of Robert Moore

Page 113: Courtesy of Robert Moore

Page 114: ASU News Service